Book Design:
    Robert Kearse Jr, Kworx Designs
    Genevieve Jackson, NU Creatrix Media

Editor:
    Shyah Dickerson, Little Engine Project

ISBN: 9798992091502

the PEACE DOCTOR'S PLAYBOOK

365 DAYS TO A STRONGER, MORE POWERFUL YOU

ERICA FORD

the PEACE DOCTOR'S PLAYBOOK:

365 DAYS TO A STRONGER, MORE POWERFUL YOU

"WELCOME TO THE START OF YOUR SEASON! THIS ISN'T JUST A JOURNAL—
IT'S YOUR PLAYBOOK FOR SUCCESS. EVERY DAY IS A CHANCE TO STEP ONTO
THE FIELD, MAKE A PLAY, AND MOVE CLOSER TO VICTORY IN YOUR LIFE.
TOGETHER, WE'LL BREAK THROUGH CHALLENGES, BUILD CONFIDENCE, AND
ELEVATE OUR GAME. THE WHISTLE HAS BLOWN, THE BALL'S IN YOUR
HANDS—LET'S MAKE THIS YEAR YOUR CHAMPIONSHIP RUN!"

This book is dedicated to all the young
people whose lives inspired every word within these pages.
Your courage, resilience, and strength light the way for all of us.

To my mother, Doris Ford, and my second mother, Viola Plummer—
thank you for never giving up on me,
for believing in my potential,
and for pushing me beyond my limits.
Your love and unwavering faith made me who I am today.

With endless gratitude and love

Blessings of Gratitude Reader,

I'm writing this book for you. Whether you are a young person navigating the challenges of growing up, a frontline organizer fighting for justice, a parent working tirelessly to provide for your family, or a corporate leader trying to inspire your team—this book is for anyone who feels overwhelmed by the noise of the world, struggling to hold onto their power and sense of direction.

The truth is, so many of us feel like we're stuck in a maze, controlled by forces outside ourselves. We often plan, dream, and hope, only to feel powerless to bring those dreams to life. We surrender to the weight of everything around us, the noise, the chaos, the relentless pressure to keep up. In those moments, it's easy to feel defeated, to feel as if we're not enough, as if we're stuck in a cycle that we can't break.

I'm here to remind you that you are powerful beyond measure. Within your own skin, your mind, your heart, and your soul, you have the strength to transform your reality. This journal is not just another book; it's a guide, an orange print, a playbook designed to help you take back control of your life and move forward with confidence, clarity, and purpose. Quotes and tools I gave my young people, families, colleagues and institutions I have worked with throughout my career.

I've spent over 37 years working with young people, families, and communities to help them find their power, to see beyond the limits the world tries to impose on them. I've witnessed the transformation that happens when someone realizes their strength, when they choose to fight for their dreams instead of surrendering to their circumstances. That's the energy I want to share with you through this book.

The Peace Doctor's Playbook is about reclaiming your life, one day at a time. It's about giving you the tools, strategies, and support you need to navigate the noise and distractions that try to pull you away from your goals. This is your daily guide to build the life you deserve—whether it's becoming more confident, finding inner peace, healing old wounds, or achieving something you've always wanted but never thought possible.

Each page in this book is a stepping stone, a daily practice designed to help you see the power within yourself. Because you are not powerless. Everything you write in this journal, every intention you set, every action you take—it's all part of building a stronger, more powerful future for yourself, your family, and your community.

Right now, we are at a pivotal time in history. It feels like the world is trying to pull us back to places we thought we had left behind. But we can't let that happen. We have come too far, individually and collectively. We have built too much, and we owe it to ourselves and those who came before us to keep moving forward. The path isn't always easy, but it's worth it. And if we don't give up, we will win.

This playbook is your companion on that journey. It's here to remind you that no matter how heavy things get, no matter how lost you might feel, you can find your way back to your own power. You have the resiliency, the tenacity, and the strength to overcome whatever life throws at you. You have the courage to keep moving, to keep building, to keep dreaming.

Every day, as you turn these pages, you'll find quotes, reflections, and action steps that are designed to help you focus, to cut through the noise, and to find the clarity you need to move forward. I encourage you to take this journey seriously, to use the tools and exercises in this book, and to tap into the community and ecosystem that this journal is part of. Together, we can help each other see the light, even in the darkest times.

This is your time. Your year. Your journey to peace, power, and purpose. Let's make it count.

With love, strength, and endless belief in you,
Erica Ford The Peace Doctor

52 Game-Changing Plays: Weekly principles to strengthen your mindset and empower your spirit.

QUARTER ONE

the
PEACE DOCTOR'S
Playbook

**"Be clear on what you want to accomplish and
the world will conspire to help you get it."**

*Success begins with a clear vision. Define your goals and understand the impact
you want to make. Clarity for me meant knowing that my mission was to save
lives and transform communities plagued by violence.*

*Write down your goals, make them specific, and revisit them often. When you
know what you're aiming for, every step you take will be purposeful and aligned
with your mission.*

Tool: Vision Board

*Create a visual representation of your goals. Include images, words, and symbols
that represent your desired outcomes. Place it somewhere you'll see it daily.*

the PEACE DOCTOR'S
*Play*book

Professional Goals for the week

- ○ _____
- ○ _____
- ○ _____
- ○ _____

Health Goals for the week

- _____ ○
- _____ ○
- _____ ○
- _____ ○

Personal Goals for the week

- ○ _____
- ○ _____
- ○ _____
- ○ _____

Love Goals for the week

- _____ ○
- _____ ○
- _____ ○
- _____ ○

Financial Goals for the week

- ○ _____
- ○ _____
- ○ _____
- ○ _____

Family Goals for the week

- _____ ○
- _____ ○
- _____ ○
- _____ ○

◉ TO START   ⊘ COMPLETED   ⊕ CONTINUE   ⊘ STUCK   ⊗ CANCEL

Day 1

_____

_____

_____

_____

_____

_____

_____

_____

Day 2

_____

_____

_____

_____

_____

_____

_____

_____

Day 3

_____
_____
_____
_____
_____
_____
_____
_____
_____

Day 4

_____
_____
_____
_____
_____
_____
_____
_____
_____

Day 5

_____

_____

_____

_____

_____

_____

_____

_____

_____

Day 6

_____

_____

_____

_____

_____

_____

_____

_____

_____

Day 7

the PEACE DOCTOR'S Playbook

"Stay focused on what you want to achieve; don't allow the noise to take you off your point"

Distractions are inevitable, but focus is key to achieving your vision. My journey involved navigating challenges from bureaucracy to street-level obstacles. Learn to prioritize tasks that directly contribute to your goals.

Tool: Daily Planner

Break down your goals into daily tasks.
Prioritize them and check them off as you complete them.

Professional Goals for the week

○ _____
○ _____
○ _____
○ _____

Health Goals for the week

_____ ○
_____ ○
_____ ○
_____ ○

Personal Goals for the week

○ _____
○ _____
○ _____
○ _____

Love Goals for the week

_____ ○
_____ ○
_____ ○
_____ ○

Financial Goals for the week

○ _____
○ _____
○ _____
○ _____

Family Goals for the week

_____ ○
_____ ○
_____ ○
_____ ○

◉ TO START   ⊘ COMPLETED   ⊖ CONTINUE   ⊘ STUCK   ⊗ CANCEL

Day 8

_____

_____

_____

_____

_____

_____

_____

_____

Day 9

_____

_____

_____

_____

_____

_____

_____

_____

Day 10

_____

_____

_____

_____

_____

_____

_____

_____

Day 11

_____

_____

_____

_____

_____

_____

_____

_____

Day 12

_____
_____
_____
_____
_____
_____
_____
_____

Day 13

_____
_____
_____
_____
_____
_____
_____
_____

Day 14

_____

_____

_____

_____

_____

_____

_____

_____

_____

the PEACE DOCTOR'S
Playbook

Week 3

"Your Word is Bond: Be Honest, Open & Above Board"

Integrity is non-negotiable. My work in violence prevention is rooted in trust and respect. Being honest and transparent in your dealings with others builds credibility and fosters trust.

Tool: Ethical Decision-Making Framework

Before making decisions, ask yourself:
Is it truthful? Is it necessary? Is it kind?

the PEACE DOCTOR'S *Play*book

Professional Goals for the week

○ _____
○ _____
○ _____
○ _____

Health Goals for the week

_____ ○
_____ ○
_____ ○
_____ ○

Personal Goals for the week

○ _____
○ _____
○ _____
○ _____

Love Goals for the week

_____ ○
_____ ○
_____ ○
_____ ○

Financial Goals for the week

○ _____
○ _____
○ _____
○ _____

Family Goals for the week

_____ ○
_____ ○
_____ ○
_____ ○

◉ TO START   ⊘ COMPLETED   ⊖ CONTINUE   ⊘ STUCK   ⊗ CANCEL

Day 15

_____

_____
_____
_____
_____
_____
_____
_____
_____

Day 16

_____

_____
_____
_____
_____
_____
_____
_____
_____

Day 17

_____
_____
_____
_____
_____
_____
_____
_____

Day 18

_____
_____
_____
_____
_____
_____
_____
_____

Day 19

_____

_____

_____

_____

_____

_____

_____

_____

Day 20

_____

_____

_____

_____

_____

_____

_____

_____

Day 21

the PEACE DOCTOR'S
Playbook

"Discipline is the bridge between goals and accomplishments."

Discipline is the backbone of achievement. I also had to be disciplined enough to put in the time to train, learn, and study so that my mission could be successful.

Tool: Accountability Partner

Pair up with someone who will keep you on track. Share your goals and check in regularly.

Professional Goals for the week

○ _____
○ _____
○ _____
○ _____

Health Goals for the week

○ _____
○ _____
○ _____
○ _____

Personal Goals for the week

○ _____
○ _____
○ _____
○ _____

Love Goals for the week

○ _____
○ _____
○ _____
○ _____

Financial Goals for the week

○ _____
○ _____
○ _____
○ _____

Family Goals for the week

○ _____
○ _____
○ _____
○ _____

◉ TO START   ⊘ COMPLETED   ⊖ CONTINUE   ⊘ STUCK   ⊗ CANCEL

Day 22

_____

_____

_____

_____

_____

_____

_____

_____

_____

Day 23

_____

_____

_____

_____

_____

_____

_____

_____

_____

Day 24

_____
_____
_____
_____
_____
_____
_____
_____
_____

Day 25

_____
_____
_____
_____
_____
_____
_____
_____
_____

Day 26

_____

_____

_____

_____

_____

_____

_____

_____

_____

Day 27

_____

_____

_____

_____

_____

_____

_____

_____

_____

Day 28

the **PEACE DOCTOR'S** *Playbook*

"Know your limitations and be honest with yourself. It's okay to seek help when you need it."

Recognize your strengths and limitations.
By being honest about your capabilities, you can seek support where needed and focus on what you do best.

Tool: SWOT Analysis

Identify your Strengths, Weaknesses, Opportunities, and Threats.

the PEACE DOCTOR'S
*Play*book

Professional Goals for the week

○ _____
○ _____
○ _____
○ _____

Health Goals for the week

_____ ○
_____ ○
_____ ○
_____ ○

Personal Goals for the week

○ _____
○ _____
○ _____
○ _____

Love Goals for the week

_____ ○
_____ ○
_____ ○
_____ ○

Financial Goals for the week

○ _____
○ _____
○ _____
○ _____

Family Goals for the week

_____ ○
_____ ○
_____ ○
_____ ○

◉ TO START   ⊘ COMPLETED   ⊖ CONTINUE   ⊘ STUCK   ⊗ CANCEL

Day 29

_____
_____
_____
_____
_____
_____
_____
_____
_____
_____

Day 30

_____
_____
_____
_____
_____
_____
_____
_____
_____
_____

Day 31

_____
_____
_____
_____
_____
_____
_____
_____

Day 32

_____
_____
_____
_____
_____
_____
_____
_____

Day 33

_____

_____

_____

_____

_____

_____

_____

_____

_____

_____

Day 34

_____

_____

_____

_____

_____

_____

_____

_____

_____

Day 35

"You don't know what you don't know, so stay humble and keep learning."

Humility is a strength. Life involves continuous learning and recognizing that there's always more to know.

Tool: Lifelong Learning Plan

Commit to regular learning, whether through courses, reading, or mentorship. Read. Read. Read.

the PEACE DOCTOR'S Playbook

Professional Goals for the week

- ○ _____
- ○ _____
- ○ _____
- ○ _____

Health Goals for the week

- ○ _____
- ○ _____
- ○ _____
- ○ _____

Personal Goals for the week

- ○ _____
- ○ _____
- ○ _____
- ○ _____

Love Goals for the week

- ○ _____
- ○ _____
- ○ _____
- ○ _____

Financial Goals for the week

- ○ _____
- ○ _____
- ○ _____
- ○ _____

Family Goals for the week

- ○ _____
- ○ _____
- ○ _____
- ○ _____

◉ TO START   ⊘ COMPLETED   ⊝ CONTINUE   ⊘ STUCK   ⊗ CANCEL

Day 36

_____

_____

_____

_____

_____

_____

_____

_____

_____

Day 37

_____

_____

_____

_____

_____

_____

_____

_____

_____

Day 38

_____
_____
_____
_____
_____
_____
_____
_____
_____

Day 39

_____
_____
_____
_____
_____
_____
_____
_____
_____

Day 40

_____

_____

_____

_____

_____

_____

_____

_____

_____

Day 41

_____

_____

_____

_____

_____

_____

_____

_____

_____

Day 42

_____

_____

_____

_____

_____

_____

_____

_____

_____

the
PEACE DOCTOR'S
Playbook

Week 7

"Study, study, study, and then study some more. Mastery requires dedication."

Mastery comes through study and practice. My impact is due to a deep understanding of the issues at hand, gained through relentless study.

Tool: Study Schedule

Dedicate time each day or week to studying.

the PEACE DOCTOR'S Playbook

Professional Goals for the week

○ _____
○ _____
○ _____
○ _____

Health Goals for the week

_____ ○
_____ ○
_____ ○
_____ ○

Personal Goals for the week

○ _____
○ _____
○ _____
○ _____

Love Goals for the week

_____ ○
_____ ○
_____ ○
_____ ○

Financial Goals for the week

○ _____
○ _____
○ _____
○ _____

Family Goals for the week

_____ ○
_____ ○
_____ ○
_____ ○

◉ TO START   ⊘ COMPLETED   ⊖ CONTINUE   ⊘ STUCK   ⊗ CANCEL

Day 43

_____
_____
_____
_____
_____
_____
_____
_____

Day 44

_____
_____
_____
_____
_____
_____
_____
_____

Day 45

_____
_____
_____
_____
_____
_____
_____
_____
_____

Day 46

_____
_____
_____
_____
_____
_____
_____
_____
_____

Day 47

Day 48

Day 49

_____

_____

_____

_____

_____

_____

_____

_____

_____

"There are no shortcuts to meaningful success."

Success is earned, not given. Your journey is one of perseverance through adversity. Understand that there are no shortcuts to meaningful change. Embrace the hard work, and take pride in the victories that come from sustained effort.

Tool: Progress Journaling

Start a process of detailing your journey, noting both the challenges and the victories in this journal every day. Reflecting on your progress

Professional Goals for the week

- ○ _____
- ○ _____
- ○ _____
- ○ _____

Health Goals for the week

- ○ _____
- ○ _____
- ○ _____
- ○ _____

Personal Goals for the week

- ○ _____
- ○ _____
- ○ _____
- ○ _____

Love Goals for the week

- ○ _____
- ○ _____
- ○ _____
- ○ _____

Financial Goals for the week

- ○ _____
- ○ _____
- ○ _____
- ○ _____

Family Goals for the week

- ○ _____
- ○ _____
- ○ _____
- ○ _____

◉ TO START   ⊘ COMPLETED   ⊖ CONTINUE   ⊘ STUCK   ⊗ CANCEL

Day 50

_____
_____
_____
_____
_____
_____
_____
_____

Day 51

_____
_____
_____
_____
_____
_____
_____
_____

Day 52

_____
_____
_____
_____
_____
_____
_____
_____

Day 53

_____
_____
_____
_____
_____
_____
_____
_____

Day 54

_____
_____
_____
_____
_____
_____
_____
_____
_____

Day 55

_____
_____
_____
_____
_____
_____
_____
_____
_____

Day 56

_____

_____

_____

_____

_____

_____

_____

_____

_____

the **PEACE DOCTOR'S**
Playbook

"The greatness within you is divinely unshakable—no earthly force can destroy it. Prosperity is knocking; step aside and let it in.
Stay focused, never give up, and always believe
in your power to achieve."

Greatness is your birthright, and no negativity can block what's meant for you. Prosperity and success are waiting, but you must make space and take action. Keep your grind tight, your focus sharper than ever, and your belief unshakable. The only person who can block your blessings is you.

Tool:
1. Street Vision Check:

Write down what's blocking your progress (negative habits, distractions, or fears). Then create a "cut-off list" to eliminate one of those obstacles each week.

2. Grind It Out Schedule:

Each morning, set a "hustle goal" for the day—whether it's sending out a resume, reaching out to a mentor, or creating a plan for your side hustle.

the
PEACE DOCTOR'S
Playbook

3. Keep Your Circle Tight:

Evaluate your crew. Are they lifting you up or dragging you down? Start spending time with people who inspire and push you to win.

4. Mirror Up Check-Up:

Look in the mirror and say out loud: "I'm ready to win. My greatness is unstoppable." Do this daily to build your confidence and mindset.

5. Prosperity Playbook:

Write out your top three goals and then identify three ways to execute each one. Cross them off as you grind through them. Progress is the goal.

Professional Goals for the week

○ _____
○ _____
○ _____
○ _____

Health Goals for the week

○ _____
○ _____
○ _____
○ _____

Personal Goals for the week

○ _____
○ _____
○ _____
○ _____

Love Goals for the week

○ _____
○ _____
○ _____
○ _____

Financial Goals for the week

○ _____
○ _____
○ _____
○ _____

Family Goals for the week

○ _____
○ _____
○ _____
○ _____

◉ TO START   ⊘ COMPLETED   ⊘ CONTINUE   ⊘ STUCK   ⊗ CANCEL

Day 57

_____
_____
_____
_____
_____
_____
_____
_____
_____

Day 58

_____
_____
_____
_____
_____
_____
_____
_____
_____

Day 59

_____
_____
_____
_____
_____
_____
_____
_____
_____

Day 60

_____
_____
_____
_____
_____
_____
_____
_____
_____

Day 61

_____

_____

_____

_____

_____

_____

_____

_____

Day 62

_____

_____

_____

_____

_____

_____

_____

_____

Day 63

_____

_____

_____

_____

_____

_____

_____

_____

_____

the PEACE DOCTOR'S Playbook

"The world is yours; live limitless."

The journey to self-actualization starts with breaking free from the limitations that have been imposed upon us—by society, by others, and most importantly, by ourselves. Your mind is like an endless river; its flow is boundless and ever-changing. Imagine a life where there are no barriers, where your dreams are not confined by what you currently see or understand. Embrace the mindset that there are no ceilings to what you can achieve. For young people, the future holds infinite possibilities—countries to explore, new skills to master, passions to discover, and heights to reach that they haven't even begun to imagine. By pushing beyond what is known and stepping into the vast potential that lies beyond, you create a life that is ever-expanding. Believe in the infinity of your abilities, and let your life be a testament to unrestrained growth and exploration.

Tool: Mindset Expansion Exercises

Regularly engage in practices that challenge your beliefs about what is possible. Start each day by writing down one limiting thought you have and reframe it into a positive, empowering statement. Set a monthly goal to step outside your comfort zone—whether it's learning a new language, visiting a new place, or trying something you've never done before. Track your experiences and reflect on how they expanded your sense of what's possible.

the PEACE DOCTOR'S Playbook

Professional Goals for the week

- ○ _____
- ○ _____
- ○ _____
- ○ _____

Health Goals for the week

- _____ ○
- _____ ○
- _____ ○
- _____ ○

Personal Goals for the week

- ○ _____
- ○ _____
- ○ _____
- ○ _____

Love Goals for the week

- _____ ○
- _____ ○
- _____ ○
- _____ ○

Financial Goals for the week

- ○ _____
- ○ _____
- ○ _____
- ○ _____

Family Goals for the week

- _____ ○
- _____ ○
- _____ ○
- _____ ○

◉ TO START   ⊘ COMPLETED   → CONTINUE   ⊘ STUCK   ⊗ CANCEL

Day 64

_____

_____

_____

_____

_____

_____

_____

_____

Day 65

_____

_____

_____

_____

_____

_____

_____

_____

Day 66

_____
_____
_____
_____
_____
_____
_____
_____
_____

Day 67

_____
_____
_____
_____
_____
_____
_____
_____
_____

Day 68

_____
_____
_____
_____
_____
_____
_____
_____
_____

Day 69

_____
_____
_____
_____
_____
_____
_____
_____
_____

Day 70

_____

_____

_____

_____

_____

_____

_____

_____

_____

the PEACE DOCTOR'S Playbook

Week 11

"Tell no lies, claim no easy victories" Amilcar Cabral

Integrity in action is critical. Your reputation is built on honesty and authenticity. Avoid exaggerating successes or hiding failures. Acknowledge the challenges you face and celebrate victories honestly. This builds credibility and long-term success.

Tool: Integrity Checklist

Before making claims or sharing information, ask yourself: Is it true? Is it earned? Use this checklist to ensure your communications are always based on truth.

Professional Goals for the week

○ _____
○ _____
○ _____
○ _____

Health Goals for the week

_____ ○
_____ ○
_____ ○
_____ ○

Personal Goals for the week

○ _____
○ _____
○ _____
○ _____

Love Goals for the week

_____ ○
_____ ○
_____ ○
_____ ○

Financial Goals for the week

○ _____
○ _____
○ _____
○ _____

Family Goals for the week

_____ ○
_____ ○
_____ ○
_____ ○

 ◉ TO START   ✓ COMPLETED   → CONTINUE   ⊘ STUCK   ⊗ CANCEL

Day 71

_____

_____

_____

_____

_____

_____

_____

_____

Peace is a
LIFESTYLE

Day 72

_____

_____

_____

_____

_____

_____

_____

_____

Day 73

_____
_____
_____
_____
_____
_____
_____
_____
_____

Day 74

_____
_____
_____
_____
_____
_____
_____
_____
_____

Day 75

_____

_____

_____

_____

_____

_____

_____

_____

Day 76

_____

_____

_____

_____

_____

_____

_____

_____

Day 77

"Lead from above by lifting others to their highest potential."

Authentic leadership is about guiding others to their highest potential. Your leadership style should be one of elevation, not domination. Lead with vision and inspire those around you to rise to their best selves. Leadership is not about control but about empowerment.

Tool: Leadership Vision Statement

Write a statement that encapsulates how you want to lead. Refer to it regularly to ensure your leadership style aligns with your highest values. Share it with your accountability partner to get insight into how you are measuring up to your vision statement.

the PEACE DOCTOR'S
Playbook

Professional Goals for the week

- ◯ _____
- ◯ _____
- ◯ _____
- ◯ _____

Health Goals for the week

- _____ ◯
- _____ ◯
- _____ ◯
- _____ ◯

Personal Goals for the week

- ◯ _____
- ◯ _____
- ◯ _____
- ◯ _____

Love Goals for the week

- _____ ◯
- _____ ◯
- _____ ◯
- _____ ◯

Financial Goals for the week

- ◯ _____
- ◯ _____
- ◯ _____
- ◯ _____

Family Goals for the week

- _____ ◯
- _____ ◯
- _____ ◯
- _____ ◯

 TO START   COMPLETED   CONTINUE   ⊘ STUCK   ⊗ CANCEL

Day 78

Day 79

Day 80

_____

_____

_____

_____

_____

_____

_____

_____

_____

Day 81

_____

_____

_____

_____

_____

_____

_____

_____

_____

Day 82

_____
_____
_____
_____
_____
_____
_____
_____

Day 83

_____
_____
_____
_____
_____
_____
_____
_____

Day 84

_____

_____

_____

_____

_____

_____

_____

_____

_____

the PEACE DOCTOR'S Playbook

"*Just because the river is quiet doesn't mean the crocodiles are gone—STAY FOCUSED! See things for what they truly are, not what your emotions paint them to be. Love life and live by the 3 R's: Respect for yourself, Respect for others, and Responsibility for your actions.*"

Life's challenges don't disappear just because things seem calm. Stay sharp, stay focused, and keep your respect game tight—for yourself, for others, and for the world around you. Your life is your masterpiece, so love it fiercely and live by a code that inspires greatness.

Tool:
1. Crocodile Check:

Each night, reflect on your day. What challenges are lying beneath the surface that you need to prepare for? Make a plan to face them head-on.

2. Emotional Filter Test:
When reacting to a situation, pause. Ask yourself, "Am I seeing this clearly, or are my emotions clouding the truth?" Write down your answers to keep yourself grounded.

the PEACE DOCTOR'S
Playbook

3. The 3 R's Challenge:

Respect for Self: *Do one thing today that prioritizes your health or well-being.*
Respect for Others: *Give genuine support or encouragement to someone in your circle.*
Responsibility: *Own your actions—whether it's an apology or stepping up to fix a mistake.*

4. Life Code Declaration:

Write your personal "Life Code" that embodies your values and goals. Read it each morning to remind yourself of the life you're building and why you love it.

Mantra:

"Love life. Stay vigilant. Respect the journey. Live by the code."

the **PEACE DOCTOR'S**
Playbook

Professional Goals for the week

- ○ _____
- ○ _____
- ○ _____
- ○ _____

Health Goals for the week

- _____ ○
- _____ ○
- _____ ○
- _____ ○

Personal Goals for the week

- ○ _____
- ○ _____
- ○ _____
- ○ _____

Love Goals for the week

- _____ ○
- _____ ○
- _____ ○
- _____ ○

Financial Goals for the week

- ○ _____
- ○ _____
- ○ _____
- ○ _____

Family Goals for the week

- _____ ○
- _____ ○
- _____ ○
- _____ ○

◉ TO START   ⊘ COMPLETED   → CONTINUE   ⊘ STUCK   ⊗ CANCEL

Day 85

_____
_____
_____
_____
_____
_____
_____
_____
_____

Day 86

_____
_____
_____
_____
_____
_____
_____
_____
_____

Day 87

_____
_____
_____
_____
_____
_____
_____
_____
_____

Day 88

_____
_____
_____
_____
_____
_____
_____
_____
_____

Day 89

_____

_____

_____

_____

_____

_____

_____

_____

_____

Day 90

_____

_____

_____

_____

_____

_____

_____

_____

_____

Day 91

_____

_____

_____

_____

_____

_____

_____

_____

the **PEACE DOCTOR'S**
Playbook

What have you accomplished? What do you still need to work on?

_____

_____

_____

_____

_____

_____

_____

_____

_____

_____

_____

_____

_____

_____

_____

_____

QUARTER TWO

"Don't move on emotions; stay grounded."

Emotions are good for understanding yourself, what moves you, what you really care about. Emotional decisions can lead to mistakes. Staying calm and centered is essential, especially in high-stakes situations. Practice emotional intelligence by recognizing and managing your emotions effectively before making decisions.

Tool: Emotional Regulation Techniques

Learn and practice techniques like deep breathing, mindfulness, and journaling to manage emotions. Use these tools to stay grounded in difficult situations. Be willing to take a moment and meditate before making decisions. Stop, Breathe, Smile, Think.

the PEACE DOCTOR'S Playbook

Professional Goals for the week

- ○ _____
- ○ _____
- ○ _____
- ○ _____

Health Goals for the week

- _____ ○
- _____ ○
- _____ ○
- _____ ○

Personal Goals for the week

- ○ _____
- ○ _____
- ○ _____
- ○ _____

Love Goals for the week

- _____ ○
- _____ ○
- _____ ○
- _____ ○

Financial Goals for the week

- ○ _____
- ○ _____
- ○ _____
- ○ _____

Family Goals for the week

- _____ ○
- _____ ○
- _____ ○
- _____ ○

 ◉ TO START   ⊘ COMPLETED   ⊖ CONTINUE   ⊘ STUCK   ⊗ CANCEL

Day 92

_____

_____

_____

_____

_____

_____

_____

_____

_____

Day 93

_____

_____

_____

_____

_____

_____

_____

_____

_____

Day 94

_____
_____
_____
_____
_____
_____
_____
_____
_____

Day 95

_____
_____
_____
_____
_____
_____
_____
_____
_____

Day 96

_____
_____
_____
_____
_____
_____
_____
_____

Peace is a
LIFESTYLE

Day 97

_____
_____
_____
_____
_____
_____
_____
_____

Day 98

_____
_____
_____
_____
_____
_____
_____
_____
_____

the PEACE DOCTOR'S Playbook

"Plan, practice, then plan and practice some more."

Success is the result of preparation and practice. Your impact is no accident; it's the result of careful planning and relentless practice. Develop a habit of planning your actions thoroughly and practicing them to perfection. Rehearse critical tasks and strategies until they become second nature.

Tool: Action Plans

For every major goal, create an action plan that outlines the steps needed to achieve it. Include timelines and practice sessions to refine your approach.

Professional Goals for the week

○ _____
○ _____
○ _____
○ _____

Health Goals for the week

_____ ○
_____ ○
_____ ○
_____ ○

Personal Goals for the week

○ _____
○ _____
○ _____
○ _____

Love Goals for the week

_____ ○
_____ ○
_____ ○
_____ ○

Financial Goals for the week

○ _____
○ _____
○ _____
○ _____

Family Goals for the week

_____ ○
_____ ○
_____ ○
_____ ○

◉ TO START   ⊘ COMPLETED   ⊕ CONTINUE   ⊘ STUCK   ⊗ CANCEL

Day 99

_____
_____
_____
_____
_____
_____
_____
_____

Day 100

_____
_____
_____
_____
_____
_____
_____
_____

Day 101

_____

_____

_____

_____

_____

_____

_____

_____

Day 102

_____

_____

_____

_____

_____

_____

_____

_____

Day 103

Day 104

Day 105

_____

_____

_____

_____

_____

_____

_____

_____

_____

the PEACE DOCTOR'S Playbook

Week 16

"Self-Care is an essential tool for your wellbeing, do not make anything more important than your wellness"

Self-care is essential for sustainable leadership. I had to learn the hard way that to be effective, I must first take care of myself. Many times I put the work ahead of everything and had to pay the consequences when my own health was compromised. Prioritize your well-being so you can be at your best when serving others. This isn't selfish—it's necessary for long-term impact.

Tool: Self-Care Plan

Develop a personalized self-care plan that includes physical, mental, and emotional well-being practices. Stick to it, even during the busiest times.Consider your sleep patterns, eating habits, exercise routine and see where you can improve. Make sure you incorporate a quarterly detox for an optimal lifestyle. Include your accountability partner.

the PEACE DOCTOR'S Playbook

Professional Goals for the week

○ _____
○ _____
○ _____
○ _____

Health Goals for the week

_____ ○
_____ ○
_____ ○
_____ ○

Personal Goals for the week

○ _____
○ _____
○ _____
○ _____

Love Goals for the week

_____ ○
_____ ○
_____ ○
_____ ○

Financial Goals for the week

○ _____
○ _____
○ _____
○ _____

Family Goals for the week

_____ ○
_____ ○
_____ ○
_____ ○

 TO START   COMPLETED   CONTINUE   ⊘ STUCK   ⊗ CANCEL

Day 106

Day 107

Day 108

_____

_____

_____

_____

_____

_____

_____

_____

Day 109

_____

_____

_____

_____

_____

_____

_____

_____

Day 110

_____
_____
_____
_____
_____
_____
_____
_____

Day 111

_____
_____
_____
_____
_____
_____
_____
_____

Day 112

"Lead with love and compassion in all things."

Leadership rooted in love is transformative. My work in violence prevention
is driven by compassion for those affected by systemic inequalities and
trauma. Leading with love means understanding and addressing the needs
of others, creating environments where people feel valued and supported.

Tool: Compassionate Leadership Practices

Implement daily acts of kindness in your leadership, such as offering support,
listening actively, and showing appreciation. Encourage a culture of
empathy within your teams.

the PEACE DOCTOR'S
*Pla*ybook

Professional Goals for the week

- _____
- _____
- _____
- _____

Health Goals for the week

- _____
- _____
- _____
- _____

Personal Goals for the week

- _____
- _____
- _____
- _____

Love Goals for the week

- _____
- _____
- _____
- _____

Financial Goals for the week

- _____
- _____
- _____
- _____

Family Goals for the week

- _____
- _____
- _____
- _____

◉ TO START   ⊘ COMPLETED   ⊖ CONTINUE   ⊘ STUCK   ⊗ CANCEL

Day 113

_____
_____
_____
_____
_____
_____
_____
_____
_____
_____

Day 114

_____
_____
_____
_____
_____
_____
_____
_____
_____

Day 115

_____
_____
_____
_____
_____
_____
_____
_____

Day 116

_____
_____
_____
_____
_____
_____
_____
_____

Day 117

_____
_____
_____
_____
_____
_____
_____
_____

Day 118

_____
_____
_____
_____
_____
_____
_____
_____

Day 119

the PEACE DOCTOR'S
*Pla*ybook

Week 18

"Hustle in silence and let your success make the noise."

The shine will come when it's time. Focus on the grind, on putting in that work to achieve your mission and vision. Don't chase the applause or the spotlight—chase the goal. The blessings, the recognition, the rewards will follow when you've done the work. It's not about showing off; it's about showing up. When you've made that impact, that's when you lift your voice, share your story, and amplify your work. Use newsletters, social media, and whatever platforms you have to tell your journey after you've achieved it. Let your results be the loudest thing in the room.

Tool: Share Your Wins Strategically
1. Work in the Shadows

Stay focused on your mission, your grind, and your growth.
Keep your head down and put in the work where it counts.

2. Amplify the Story After the Win

Once you've reached your milestones, then it's time to share. Use newsletters, social media, or events to uplift the voices of your organization, your team, and even your kids. Let your story inspire others once you've walked the path.

3. Let Success Speak for Itself

When you achieve, let that success do the talking.
The shine is coming—just be patient and keep grinding.

the PEACE DOCTOR'S
*Pla*book

Professional Goals for the week

- ○ _____
- ○ _____
- ○ _____
- ○ _____

Health Goals for the week

- _____ ○
- _____ ○
- _____ ○
- _____ ○

Personal Goals for the week

- ○ _____
- ○ _____
- ○ _____
- ○ _____

Love Goals for the week

- _____ ○
- _____ ○
- _____ ○
- _____ ○

Financial Goals for the week

- ○ _____
- ○ _____
- ○ _____
- ○ _____

Family Goals for the week

- _____ ○
- _____ ○
- _____ ○
- _____ ○

◉ TO START   ⊘ COMPLETED   ⊝ CONTINUE   ⊘ STUCK   ⊗ CANCEL

Day 120

Day 121

Day 122

_____
_____
_____
_____
_____
_____
_____
_____
_____

Day 123

_____
_____
_____
_____
_____
_____
_____
_____
_____

Day 124

_____
_____
_____
_____
_____
_____
_____
_____
_____

Peace is a
LIFESTYLE

Day 125

_____
_____
_____
_____
_____
_____
_____
_____
_____

Day 126

_____

_____

_____

_____

_____

_____

_____

_____

_____

the PEACE DOCTOR'S Playbook

"Adopt the mentality that challenges are happening for you, not to you"

Shift from a victim mindset to one of empowerment. Life's challenges can be opportunities for growth and learning if you approach them with the right mindset. By viewing experiences as happening for your benefit, rather than as something inflicted upon you, you reclaim your power and agency.

Tool: Reframing Practice

When faced with a challenge, consciously reframe it as an opportunity. Ask yourself: What can I learn from this? How can this help me grow? Write down your reflections to reinforce this mindset shift.

the PEACE DOCTOR'S Playbook

Professional Goals for the week

○ _____
○ _____
○ _____
○ _____

Health Goals for the week

○ _____
○ _____
○ _____
○ _____

Personal Goals for the week

○ _____
○ _____
○ _____
○ _____

Love Goals for the week

○ _____
○ _____
○ _____
○ _____

Financial Goals for the week

○ _____
○ _____
○ _____
○ _____

Family Goals for the week

○ _____
○ _____
○ _____
○ _____

◉ TO START   ⊘ COMPLETED   ⊖ CONTINUE   ⊘ STUCK   ⊗ CANCEL

Day 127

_____
_____
_____
_____
_____
_____
_____
_____

Day 128

_____
_____
_____
_____
_____
_____
_____
_____

Day 129

_____
_____
_____
_____
_____
_____
_____
_____
_____
_____

Day 130

_____
_____
_____
_____
_____
_____
_____
_____
_____
_____

Day 131

_____
_____
_____
_____
_____
_____
_____
_____

Day 132

_____
_____
_____
_____
_____
_____
_____
_____

Day 133

_____

_____

_____

_____

_____

_____

_____

_____

_____

the PEACE DOCTOR'S Playbook

"Be great, don't settle for mediocrity"

Strive for excellence in everything you do. Refuse to settle for mediocrity, knowing that your best effort is required to achieve the change you seek. Excellence should be your standard in all aspects of your life and work.

Tool: Excellence Tracking

Set personal and professional standards for excellence. Create a system to track your progress, evaluate your efforts, and continually raise the bar. Celebrate achievements, but always look for ways to improve.

the PEACE DOCTOR'S Playbook

Professional Goals for the week

- ◯ _____
- ◯ _____
- ◯ _____
- ◯ _____

Health Goals for the week

- ◯ _____
- ◯ _____
- ◯ _____
- ◯ _____

Personal Goals for the week

- ◯ _____
- ◯ _____
- ◯ _____
- ◯ _____

Love Goals for the week

- ◯ _____
- ◯ _____
- ◯ _____
- ◯ _____

Financial Goals for the week

- ◯ _____
- ◯ _____
- ◯ _____
- ◯ _____

Family Goals for the week

- ◯ _____
- ◯ _____
- ◯ _____
- ◯ _____

◉ TO START   ⊘ COMPLETED   ⊝ CONTINUE   ⊘ STUCK   ⊗ CANCEL

Day 134

Day 135

Day 136

Day 137

Day 138

Day 139

Day 140

_____
_____
_____
_____
_____
_____
_____
_____
_____

the PEACE DOCTOR'S
Playbook

Week 21

"Don't try to get over, operate with integrity always"

Integrity means doing the right thing, even when it's difficult. Choose honesty and hard work over shortcuts or unethical behavior. Trying to "get over" or take shortcuts may offer temporary gains, but it undermines trust and long-term success.

Tool: Ethical Decision-Making Checklist

Before making decisions, especially tough ones, review a checklist that includes questions like: Is this fair? Does this align with my values? Will this build trust? Use it to guide your actions and ensure you're always operating with integrity.

Professional Goals for the week

○ _____
○ _____
○ _____
○ _____

Health Goals for the week

○ _____
○ _____
○ _____
○ _____

Personal Goals for the week

○ _____
○ _____
○ _____
○ _____

Love Goals for the week

○ _____
○ _____
○ _____
○ _____

Financial Goals for the week

○ _____
○ _____
○ _____
○ _____

Family Goals for the week

○ _____
○ _____
○ _____
○ _____

◉ TO START   ⊘ COMPLETED   ⊙ CONTINUE   ⊘ STUCK   ⊗ CANCEL

Day 141

_____

_____

_____

_____

_____

_____

_____

_____

Day 142

_____

_____

_____

_____

_____

_____

_____

_____

Day 143

_____

_____

_____

_____

_____

_____

_____

_____

_____

_____

Day 144

_____

_____

_____

_____

_____

_____

_____

_____

_____

_____

Day 145

Day 146

Day 147

the PEACE DOCTOR'S
*Play*book

"Focus on your process, not just the outcome the journey matters"

The journey is just as important as the destination. Focusing too much on the outcome can lead to frustration and burnout. By valuing the process—the learning, growth, and relationships built along the way—you ensure sustainable success and fulfillment.

Tool: Process Journaling

Use your journal where you document not just your goals but the steps you're taking to achieve them. Reflect on what you're learning and how you're growing throughout the process, not just on the end results.

the PEACE DOCTOR'S
*Pla*book

Professional Goals for the week

- ◯ ....
- ◯ ....
- ◯ ....
- ◯ ....

Health Goals for the week

- .... ◯
- .... ◯
- .... ◯
- .... ◯

Personal Goals for the week

- ◯ ....
- ◯ ....
- ◯ ....
- ◯ ....

Love Goals for the week

- .... ◯
- .... ◯
- .... ◯
- .... ◯

Financial Goals for the week

- ◯ ....
- ◯ ....
- ◯ ....
- ◯ ....

Family Goals for the week

- .... ◯
- .... ◯
- .... ◯
- .... ◯

◉ TO START   ⊘ COMPLETED   ⊖ CONTINUE   ⊘ STUCK   ⊗ CANCEL

Week 22

Day 148

Day 149

Day 150

Day 151

Day 152

Day 153

Day 154

the **PEACE** **DOCTOR'S**
Playbook

Week 23

"Protect your peace by guarding your mental and emotional wellbeing"

Guard your mental and emotional well-being fiercely. Maintaining inner peace is essential to your ability to lead and serve effectively. Set boundaries, prioritize self-care, and remove yourself from toxic environments or relationships that threaten your peace.

Tool: Peace Inventory

Regularly assess the people, activities, and environments in your life. Determine what contributes to your peace and what disrupts it. Make necessary adjustments to prioritize activities and relationships that nurture your well-being.

Professional Goals for the week

○ _____
○ _____
○ _____
○ _____

Health Goals for the week

○ _____
○ _____
○ _____
○ _____

Personal Goals for the week

○ _____
○ _____
○ _____
○ _____

Love Goals for the week

○ _____
○ _____
○ _____
○ _____

Financial Goals for the week

○ _____
○ _____
○ _____
○ _____

Family Goals for the week

○ _____
○ _____
○ _____
○ _____

◉ TO START   ⊘ COMPLETED   ⊙ CONTINUE   ⊘ STUCK   ⊗ CANCEL

Day 155

_____
_____
_____
_____
_____
_____
_____
_____

Day 156

_____
_____
_____
_____
_____
_____
_____
_____

Day 157

_____

_____

_____

_____

_____

_____

_____

_____

_____

Day 158

_____

_____

_____

_____

_____

_____

_____

_____

_____

Day 159

_____

_____

_____

_____

_____

_____

_____

_____

Day 160

_____

_____

_____

_____

_____

_____

_____

_____

Day 161

"Communicate with clarity; say what you mean and ensure others understand."

Effective communication is the foundation of strong relationships, leadership, and collaboration. To prevent misunderstandings, be clear, concise, and transparent in your words. Speak with honesty, leaving no room for misinterpretation. Make it a habit to confirm that those you communicate with truly understand your message. Whether it's your team, children, or community, ensure that everyone is on the same page. Clear communication isn't just about speaking—it's about listening, confirming, and aligning to avoid assumptions. When everyone understands your message, it leads to better outcomes, stronger trust, and smoother collaboration.

Tool: Clarity Check Exercise

At the end of every conversation or meeting, ask the person to repeat what they understood. This simple exercise ensures alignment and confirms that your message was received as intended. Use it regularly with your team, family, or any group you lead.

Tool: Active Listening Workshops

Organize or participate in workshops focused on improving communication skills, emphasizing active listening, non-verbal cues, and precise language. Practice checking for understanding and refine your ability to articulate your thoughts clearly.

the PEACE DOCTOR'S
*Pla*ybook

Professional Goals for the week

- ○ _____ ○
- ○ _____ ○
- ○ _____ ○
- ○ _____ ○

Health Goals for the week

Personal Goals for the week

- ○ _____ ○
- ○ _____ ○
- ○ _____ ○
- ○ _____ ○

Love Goals for the week

Financial Goals for the week

- ○ _____ ○
- ○ _____ ○
- ○ _____ ○
- ○ _____ ○

Family Goals for the week

 TO START   ⊘ COMPLETED   ⊖ CONTINUE   ⊘ STUCK   ⊗ CANCEL

Day 162

_____
_____
_____
_____
_____
_____
_____
_____
_____

Day 163

_____
_____
_____
_____
_____
_____
_____
_____
_____

Day 164

Day 165

Day 166

_____
_____
_____
_____
_____
_____
_____
_____

Day 167

_____
_____
_____
_____
_____
_____
_____
_____

Day 168

_____

_____

_____

_____

_____

_____

_____

_____

_____

"Release judgment, envy, and jealousy; embrace openness and celebrate the success of others."

Judgment, envy, and jealousy create barriers to meaningful connections and personal growth. Instead of comparing yourself to others or forming quick judgments, approach people and situations with openness, curiosity, and appreciation. Recognize that everyone has a unique journey, and your path is yours alone. By releasing envy and jealousy, you open yourself up to celebrate the successes of others and to focus on your own growth. This mindset shift fosters deeper, more positive interactions and creates a spirit of mutual respect and genuine support. Embrace a life free of comparisons, filled with gratitude, and rooted in self-confidence.

Tool: Non-Judgmental Communication Practice

Engage in conversations with a focus on listening without immediate judgment. Reflect back on what you hear to ensure understanding and respond thoughtfully. This practice fosters a culture of respect and openness in your relationships.

Tool: Daily Gratitude and Self-Confidence Journaling

Every day, write down something you're grateful for and one accomplishment you're proud of. Reflect on the unique strengths and progress in your journey. This practice shifts your focus from comparison to appreciation, building self-confidence and a positive mindset.

Professional Goals for the week

○ _____
○ _____
○ _____
○ _____

Health Goals for the week

○ _____
○ _____
○ _____
○ _____

Personal Goals for the week

○ _____
○ _____
○ _____
○ _____

Love Goals for the week

○ _____
○ _____
○ _____
○ _____

Financial Goals for the week

○ _____
○ _____
○ _____
○ _____

Family Goals for the week

○ _____
○ _____
○ _____
○ _____

◉ TO START   ⊘ COMPLETED   ⊙ CONTINUE   ⊘ STUCK   ⊗ CANCEL

Day 169

_____
_____
_____
_____
_____
_____
_____
_____

Day 170

_____
_____
_____
_____
_____
_____
_____
_____

Day 171

_____
_____
_____
_____
_____
_____
_____
_____
_____

Day 172

_____
_____
_____
_____
_____
_____
_____
_____
_____

Day 173

Day 174

Day 175

_____

_____

_____

_____

_____

_____

_____

_____

_____

the PEACE DOCTOR'S Playbook

"Believe in something greater than yourself; let faith guide you."

We are spiritual beings navigating a human world, and to thrive, we must remain centered and grounded. Faith in something beyond yourself—whether it's a spiritual belief, ancestral wisdom, or a higher purpose—it provides strength, humility, and direction. It reminds you that you are not all-powerful and that there are forces beyond your control working in your favor. This belief brings resilience, helping you navigate challenges with grace, knowing that you are supported by something greater. Trust in this guidance, and you will find the courage to move forward, accomplish your goals, and make an impact that transcends the immediate.

Tool: Spiritual/Philosophical Reflection

Dedicate time each day for reflection to connect with your higher purpose. Engage in activities like prayer, meditation, or music to ground and center you. Consider writing in your journal about your beliefs and how they guide your actions. This practice helps align your actions with your deeper values and provides strength in difficult times, as well as keeps you humble.

the PEACE DOCTOR'S
*Pla*book

Professional Goals for the week

○ _____
○ _____
○ _____
○ _____

Health Goals for the week

_____ ○
_____ ○
_____ ○
_____ ○

Personal Goals for the week

○ _____
○ _____
○ _____
○ _____

Love Goals for the week

_____ ○
_____ ○
_____ ○
_____ ○

Financial Goals for the week

○ _____
○ _____
○ _____
○ _____

Family Goals for the week

_____ ○
_____ ○
_____ ○
_____ ○

 TO START   COMPLETED   CONTINUE   ⊘ STUCK   ⊗ CANCEL

Day 176

_____
_____
_____
_____
_____
_____
_____
_____
_____

Day 177

_____
_____
_____
_____
_____
_____
_____
_____
_____

Day 178

_____

_____

_____

_____

_____

_____

_____

_____

Day 179

_____

_____

_____

_____

_____

_____

_____

_____

Day 180

_____
_____
_____
_____
_____
_____
_____
_____
_____

Peace is a
LIFESTYLE

Day 181

_____
_____
_____
_____
_____
_____
_____
_____
_____

Day 182

_____

_____

_____

_____

_____

_____

_____

_____

_____

the PEACE DOCTOR'S Playbook

What have you accomplished? What do you still need to work on?

_____

_____

_____

_____

_____

_____

_____

_____

_____

_____

_____

_____

_____

_____

_____

Peace is a LIFESTYLE

QUARTER THREE

the PEACE DOCTOR'S Playbook

**"Peace begins within, for it is the harmony
inside that transforms the world outside."**

*True peace isn't just about silencing the chaos around us; it's about quieting the
storm within. When we cultivate inner peace, we radiate calm, resilience, and
strength into our communities. To make peace a lifestyle, it starts with how we
speak to ourselves. By nurturing a positive internal dialogue, we empower
ourselves to lead with love and compassion.*

Tools:
1. Inner Dialogue Journal

*Document your internal thoughts daily. Capture moments of negativity and
consciously counter them with affirmations that uplift and inspire. This exercise
helps reframe your mindset, fostering a powerful shift toward positivity.*

2. Self-Talk Tracker

*Throughout your day, take note of your internal dialogue. For every self-critical
thought, replace it with a self-compassionate statement. By consistently monitoring
and adjusting your self-talk, you'll build a habit of inner kindness that strengthens
your resolve to live peacefully.*

*These tools are simple but transformative practices to make peace a constant state
of being, allowing us to heal ourselves and, ultimately, our communities.*

the PEACE DOCTOR'S
_Pla_ybook

Professional Goals for the week

○ _____
○ _____
○ _____
○ _____

Health Goals for the week

_____ ○
_____ ○
_____ ○
_____ ○

Personal Goals for the week

○ _____
○ _____
○ _____
○ _____

Love Goals for the week

_____ ○
_____ ○
_____ ○
_____ ○

Financial Goals for the week

○ _____
○ _____
○ _____
○ _____

Family Goals for the week

_____ ○
_____ ○
_____ ○
_____ ○

◉ TO START   ⊘ COMPLETED   ⊖ CONTINUE   ⊘ STUCK   ⊗ CANCEL

Day 183

_____
_____
_____
_____
_____
_____
_____
_____

Day 184

_____
_____
_____
_____
_____
_____
_____
_____

Day 185

_____
_____
_____
_____
_____
_____
_____
_____
_____

Day 186

_____
_____
_____
_____
_____
_____
_____
_____
_____

Day 187

_____
_____
_____
_____
_____
_____
_____
_____

Day 188

_____
_____
_____
_____
_____
_____
_____
_____

Day 189

the PEACE DOCTOR'S Playbook

"There is no success without sacrifice. Choose your sacrifices wisely, for they determine your path."

Success is not an overnight achievement; it is the result of dedication, commitment, and sacrifice. To reach your highest potential, you must be willing to invest time, energy, and effort in the right places. Whether it's letting go of habits that hold you back or prioritizing your goals over temporary pleasures, progress requires thoughtful sacrifices. However, not all sacrifices are created equal—what you give up should align with your values and long-term vision. Remember, what you put into the world is what you get back. If you want greatness, you must be prepared to commit fully.

Tool: Mindset Reset for Sacrifice

True sacrifice starts in the mind—it's not just about what you give up but how you prepare yourself mentally to release it. This tool helps you cultivate the inner strength to align your sacrifices with your deepest values. Before letting go of anything external, you need to prepare your mind to see sacrifice not as loss, but as a powerful investment in your future self.

the **PEACE DOCTOR'S**
*Pla*ybook

Week 28

Action Plan:
1. Mindset Meditation

Begin each day with 5-10 minutes of meditation focused on the idea of purposeful sacrifice. Visualize your biggest goals and feel the empowerment that comes with releasing what no longer serves you. This daily practice will help you develop a mindset where sacrifice feels like growth, not deprivation.

2. Sacrifice Affirmations

Write down affirmations like "I am choosing to release what holds me back," or "Every sacrifice I make is a step toward my vision." Repeat these throughout your day to remind yourself that you are in control of what you give up and why.

3. Internal Reframe Journal

At the end of this week, document what you chose to let go of—whether it was a habit, a distraction, or even a mindset. Reflect on how these sacrifices have cleared space for your growth. This will train your mind to view sacrifice not as losing something, but as making room for what truly matters.

By focusing on your mindset, this tool will transform the concept of sacrifice into a positive, empowering force that pushes you forward with purpose and clarity.

the PEACE DOCTOR'S
Playbook

Professional Goals for the week

- ○ _____
- ○ _____
- ○ _____
- ○ _____

Health Goals for the week

- _____ ○
- _____ ○
- _____ ○
- _____ ○

Personal Goals for the week

- ○ _____
- ○ _____
- ○ _____
- ○ _____

Love Goals for the week

- _____ ○
- _____ ○
- _____ ○
- _____ ○

Financial Goals for the week

- ○ _____
- ○ _____
- ○ _____
- ○ _____

Family Goals for the week

- _____ ○
- _____ ○
- _____ ○
- _____ ○

◉ TO START ⊘ COMPLETED → CONTINUE ⊘ STUCK ⊗ CANCEL

Day 190

_____
_____
_____
_____
_____
_____
_____
_____

Day 191

_____
_____
_____
_____
_____
_____
_____
_____

Day 192

_____
_____
_____
_____
_____
_____
_____
_____
_____

Day 193

_____
_____
_____
_____
_____
_____
_____
_____
_____

Day 194

_____

_____

_____

_____

_____

_____

_____

_____

Day 195

_____

_____

_____

_____

_____

_____

_____

_____

Day 196

_____

_____

_____

_____

_____

_____

_____

_____

_____

"Expand Your Worldview, there's always more to learn"

Broaden your perspective to enrich your life and work. The world is vast, with diverse experiences and knowledge to offer. By expanding your worldview, you open yourself to new ideas, cultures, and opportunities that can enhance your effectiveness and empathy.

Tool: Cross-Cultural Engagement

Actively seek out experiences that broaden your understanding of different cultures and perspectives. This could be through travel, reading diverse literature, attending cultural events, or engaging with different communities.

Professional Goals for the week

- ○ _____
- ○ _____
- ○ _____
- ○ _____

Health Goals for the week

- ○ _____
- ○ _____
- ○ _____
- ○ _____

Personal Goals for the week

- ○ _____
- ○ _____
- ○ _____
- ○ _____

Love Goals for the week

- ○ _____
- ○ _____
- ○ _____
- ○ _____

Financial Goals for the week

- ○ _____
- ○ _____
- ○ _____
- ○ _____

Family Goals for the week

- ○ _____
- ○ _____
- ○ _____
- ○ _____

◉ TO START　⊘ COMPLETED　⊖ CONTINUE　⊘ STUCK　⊗ CANCEL

Day 197

_____
_____
_____
_____
_____
_____
_____
_____
_____

Day 198

_____
_____
_____
_____
_____
_____
_____
_____
_____

Day 199

_____
_____
_____
_____
_____
_____
_____
_____
_____

Day 200

_____
_____
_____
_____
_____
_____
_____
_____
_____

Day 201

_____

Day 202

_____

Day 203

_____

_____

_____

_____

_____

_____

_____

_____

_____

the **PEACE** **DOCTOR'S**
Playbook

Week 30

**"The World did not start with you,
pay homage to those that came before you"**

*Recognize and honor the contributions of those who paved the way. Your
work is built on the legacy of countless individuals who fought for peace and
justice before you. You are a continuation of what came before you.
Understand that you are part of a larger continuum, and pay homage to
those before you give your work depth and context.*

Tool: Legacy Reflection

*Study the history of your field or community and acknowledge the pioneers
who came before you. Incorporate lessons from their experiences into your
own work and consider how you can contribute to this ongoing legacy.*

Professional Goals for the week

- ○ _____
- ○ _____
- ○ _____
- ○ _____

Health Goals for the week

- _____ ○
- _____ ○
- _____ ○
- _____ ○

Personal Goals for the week

- ○ _____
- ○ _____
- ○ _____
- ○ _____

Love Goals for the week

- _____ ○
- _____ ○
- _____ ○
- _____ ○

Financial Goals for the week

- ○ _____
- ○ _____
- ○ _____
- ○ _____

Family Goals for the week

- _____ ○
- _____ ○
- _____ ○
- _____ ○

◉ TO START   ⊘ COMPLETED   ⊖ CONTINUE   ⊘ STUCK   ⊗ CANCEL

Day 204

_____
_____
_____
_____
_____
_____
_____
_____

Day 205

_____
_____
_____
_____
_____
_____
_____
_____

Day 206

_____
_____
_____
_____
_____
_____
_____
_____
_____

Day 207

_____
_____
_____
_____
_____
_____
_____
_____
_____

Day 208

_____
_____
_____
_____
_____
_____
_____
_____

Day 209

_____
_____
_____
_____
_____
_____
_____
_____

Day 210

_____

_____

_____

_____

_____

_____

_____

_____

_____

the
Playbook
PEACE DOCTOR'S

Week 31

"Movement is medicine, stay active to maintain your vitality"

Physical movement is not just about health—it's about vitality and resilience. Incorporating physical activity into your routine is a way to stay energized, reduce stress, and maintain a positive outlook. Movement keeps you grounded and connected to your body, which is essential for mental and emotional well-being.

Tool: Regular Exercise Routine

Develop a regular exercise routine that you enjoy, whether it's walking, dancing, yoga, or another form of movement. Incorporate it into your daily or weekly schedule as a non-negotiable part of your self-care.

the PEACE DOCTOR'S
Playbook

Professional Goals for the week

○ _____
○ _____
○ _____
○ _____

Health Goals for the week

○ _____
○ _____
○ _____
○ _____

Personal Goals for the week

○ _____
○ _____
○ _____
○ _____

Love Goals for the week

○ _____
○ _____
○ _____
○ _____

Financial Goals for the week

○ _____
○ _____
○ _____
○ _____

Family Goals for the week

○ _____
○ _____
○ _____
○ _____

◉ TO START   ⊘ COMPLETED   → CONTINUE   ⊘ STUCK   ⊗ CANCEL

Day 211

_____
_____
_____
_____
_____
_____
_____
_____
_____

Day 212

_____
_____
_____
_____
_____
_____
_____
_____
_____

Day 213

_____

_____

_____

_____

_____

_____

_____

_____

_____

Day 214

_____

_____

_____

_____

_____

_____

_____

_____

_____

Day 215

_____
_____
_____
_____
_____
_____
_____
_____

Day 216

_____
_____
_____
_____
_____
_____
_____
_____

Day 217

Week 32

"Turn your pain into power by using it to fuel your purpose."

Pain is inevitable, but it doesn't have to break you. Instead, let it build you. Every setback, every loss—use them as fuel to push forward. When life knocks you down, let that fire in your soul drive you toward your dreams. Carry the strength of your struggles with you, transforming pain into purpose.

Tool: Pain to Purpose Worksheet
1. Reflect & Write

List your biggest challenges and losses.
Acknowledge how they made you feel.

2. Reframe

For each experience, identify one way you can turn it into a strength or use it to help others.

3. Affirm & Visualize
Create affirmations like, "My pain fuels my growth."

Visualize turning your struggles into the fire that drives your purpose.

the PEACE DOCTOR'S
*Pla*ybook

Professional Goals for the week

○ _____ ○
○ _____ ○
○ _____ ○
○ _____ ○

Health Goals for the week

○ _____ ○
○ _____ ○
○ _____ ○
○ _____ ○

Personal Goals for the week

○ _____ ○
○ _____ ○
○ _____ ○
○ _____ ○

Love Goals for the week

○ _____ ○
○ _____ ○
○ _____ ○
○ _____ ○

Financial Goals for the week

○ _____ ○
○ _____ ○
○ _____ ○
○ _____ ○

Family Goals for the week

○ _____ ○
○ _____ ○
○ _____ ○
○ _____ ○

◉ TO START   ⊘ COMPLETED   ⊖ CONTINUE   ⊘ STUCK   ⊗ CANCEL

Day 218

_____

_____

_____

_____

_____

_____

_____

_____

Day 219

_____

_____

_____

_____

_____

_____

_____

_____

Day 220

_____
_____
_____
_____
_____
_____
_____
_____
_____
_____

Day 221

_____
_____
_____
_____
_____
_____
_____
_____
_____
_____

Day 222

_____
_____
_____
_____
_____
_____
_____
_____
_____

Day 223

_____
_____
_____
_____
_____
_____
_____
_____
_____

Day 224

_____

_____

_____

_____

_____

_____

_____

_____

_____

the
PEACE DOCTOR'S
Playbook

Week 33

"Death is not if but when. But it's not the day someone leaves us that defines them—it's the legacy they built, the love they gave, and the impact they had. We honor them by keeping their spirit alive in how we live, love, and remember."

Life's most meaningful work is preserving the legacy of those we love. The Peace Doctor's Playbook equips you with the tools to honor their memory—not just in grief, but through action. This is your guide to turning pain into purpose and creating a life filled with peace, love, and unforgettable impact.

Tool:
Legacy Journaling:

Reflect on and document the lessons, love, and memories shared with loved ones.

Memory Builders:

Create traditions, share stories, or build projects that celebrate their lives.

Living Tributes:

Carry forward their values and vision in your daily life and within your community.

Connection Exercises:

Strengthen your relationships today to create legacies that last tomorrow.

Professional Goals for the week

○ _____
○ _____
○ _____
○ _____

Health Goals for the week

_____ ○
_____ ○
_____ ○
_____ ○

Personal Goals for the week

○ _____
○ _____
○ _____
○ _____

Love Goals for the week

_____ ○
_____ ○
_____ ○
_____ ○

Financial Goals for the week

○ _____
○ _____
○ _____
○ _____

Family Goals for the week

_____ ○
_____ ○
_____ ○
_____ ○

◉ TO START   ⊘ COMPLETED   ⊖ CONTINUE   ⊘ STUCK   ⊗ CANCEL

Day 225

_____
_____
_____
_____
_____
_____
_____
_____
_____

Peace is a
LIFESTYLE

Day 226

_____
_____
_____
_____
_____
_____
_____
_____
_____

Day 227

_____

_____

_____

_____

_____

_____

_____

_____

_____

Day 228

_____

_____

_____

_____

_____

_____

_____

_____

_____

Day 229

Day 230

Day 231

_____

_____

_____

_____

_____

_____

_____

_____

_____

the PEACE DOCTOR'S Playbook

"When you've got nothing left, tap in.
Let your resilience and tenacity show up."

When you're down to your last dollar, facing eviction, or when no one's hearing your cries—these are the moments that test your spirit. It's in these times that you've got to dig deep, tap into your inner strength, and refuse to give up. I have lived through these struggles, facing what seemed impossible and still standing strong. I know what it means to survive against all odds, to fight when there's nothing left but the will to keep going. We are a people who refuse to break, who turn pain into power and challenge into change. Share your story, write your book, teach your resilience—because in telling our stories, we breathe life into each other's journeys.

Tool: Tap-In Resilience Practice
1. Reflect & Write

When you're feeling defeated, write down a time when you faced a tough situation and pushed through. Let those memories remind you of your inner strength.

2. Daily Mantra

Use affirmations like, "I am resilient. I am unbreakable.
I will rise," to center yourself when everything feels impossible.

3. Breathe & Ground

Take a moment to breathe deeply, ground yourself, and reconnect with your purpose. Remind yourself that just like Erica, you have the power to push through and transform your story.

the PEACE DOCTOR'S Playbook

Professional Goals for the week

○ _____
○ _____
○ _____
○ _____

Health Goals for the week

○ _____
○ _____
○ _____
○ _____

Personal Goals for the week

○ _____
○ _____
○ _____
○ _____

Love Goals for the week

○ _____
○ _____
○ _____
○ _____

Financial Goals for the week

○ _____
○ _____
○ _____
○ _____

Family Goals for the week

○ _____
○ _____
○ _____
○ _____

◉ TO START   ⊘ COMPLETED   ⊖ CONTINUE   ⊘ STUCK   ⊗ CANCEL

Day 232

_____
_____
_____
_____
_____
_____
_____
_____

Day 233

_____
_____
_____
_____
_____
_____
_____
_____

Day 234

_____

_____

_____

_____

_____

_____

_____

_____

Day 235

_____

_____

_____

_____

_____

_____

_____

_____

Day 236

Day 237

Day 238

the **PEACE DOCTOR'S** *Playbook*

"Release judgment, approach others with openness"

Judgment only puts up walls. When we judge others too quickly, we miss out on the chance to connect, to truly understand, and to build something real together. We can't grow if we're busy shutting people out. Let go of those assumptions and approach every interaction with an open mind. When we release judgment, we make space for real dialogue, real healing, and real change.

Tool: Non-Judgmental Communication Practice
1. Listen First

The next time someone speaks, slow down. Don't rush to conclusions. Just listen. Be fully present, letting their words sink in before you respond.

2. Reflect Back

After listening, repeat back what you heard to make sure you understood them. This shows respect and creates space for honest conversation.

3. Respond with Curiosity

Instead of reacting defensively or shutting down, ask questions. Be genuinely curious about their perspective. This opens doors for deeper connection and mutual growth. When we let go of judgment, we build stronger communities rooted in trust and understanding.

Professional Goals for the week

○ _____
○ _____
○ _____
○ _____

Health Goals for the week

○ _____
○ _____
○ _____
○ _____

Personal Goals for the week

○ _____
○ _____
○ _____
○ _____

Love Goals for the week

○ _____
○ _____
○ _____
○ _____

Financial Goals for the week

○ _____
○ _____
○ _____
○ _____

Family Goals for the week

○ _____
○ _____
○ _____
○ _____

◉ TO START   ⊘ COMPLETED   ⊖ CONTINUE   ⊘ STUCK   ⊗ CANCEL

Day 239

_____
_____
_____
_____
_____
_____
_____
_____
_____

Day 240

_____
_____
_____
_____
_____
_____
_____
_____
_____

Day 241

_____
_____
_____
_____
_____
_____
_____
_____
_____

Day 242

_____
_____
_____
_____
_____
_____
_____
_____
_____

Day 243

Day 244

Day 245

_____

_____

_____

_____

_____

_____

_____

_____

_____

_____

**"The most important conversations
are the ones you have with yourself."**

You can have the most powerful vision, the greatest idea—but if your inner voice is filled with doubt, you'll pop your own dreams before they even take flight. Too often, we let that negative self-talk deflate our spirit, kill our goals, and keep us stuck. It's time to get out of your own head and step into your power. You're not your past, not the mistakes of yesterday, not bound by your family's history. You are incomparable, you are great, and you have the power to break every cycle that stands in your way.

Tool: Self-Talk Assessment
1. Check Your Thoughts

Take a moment each day to notice your inner dialogue. Are you lifting yourself up, or tearing yourself down? Write down any negative thoughts you catch.

2. Flip the Script

For every self-critical thought, write a compassionate statement to replace it. Remind yourself: "I am strong. I am capable. I am becoming better every day."

3. Boost Your Mindset

*Meditate, listen to a positive playlist, or surround yourself with people who elevate you. Keep your mind filled with affirmations and positivity.
Your reality shifts when your self-talk shifts.*

The PEACE DOCTOR'S Playbook

Professional Goals for the week

- _____
- _____
- _____
- _____

Health Goals for the week

- _____
- _____
- _____
- _____

Personal Goals for the week

- _____
- _____
- _____
- _____

Love Goals for the week

- _____
- _____
- _____
- _____

Financial Goals for the week

- _____
- _____
- _____
- _____

Family Goals for the week

- _____
- _____
- _____
- _____

⊙ TO START　　⊘ COMPLETED　　⊖ CONTINUE　　⊘ STUCK　　⊗ CANCEL

Day 246

_____

_____

_____

_____

_____

_____

_____

_____

Day 247

_____

_____

_____

_____

_____

_____

_____

_____

Day 248

_____
_____
_____
_____
_____
_____
_____
_____
_____

Day 249

_____
_____
_____
_____
_____
_____
_____
_____
_____

Day 250

_____
_____
_____
_____
_____
_____
_____
_____

Day 251

_____
_____
_____
_____
_____
_____
_____
_____

Day 252

_____

_____

_____

_____

_____

_____

_____

_____

_____

the PEACE DOCTOR'S Playbook

Week 37

**"Don't let fear decide your future.
Be courageous in the face of uncertainty."**

Fear is everywhere—fear of failing, not being seen, losing it all. But here's the truth: if I let fear stop me, LIFE Camp wouldn't exist, and we wouldn't be saving lives or building peace. Fear is just a bully trying to keep you small. You've got to face it, push past it, and let your courage and faith guide you. Courage doesn't mean fear disappears—it means you move forward anyway.

Tool: Fear-Setting Worksheet
1. Name the Fear

*Write down what's holding you back.
Get it out of your head and onto paper.*

2. Plan to Act

*For each fear, write one step to face it.
How can you prevent it or bounce back if it happens?*

3. Push Through

*Focus on your vision. Imagine what happens when you win despite the fear.
Use that fire to keep moving forward—unstoppable.*

Professional Goals for the week

○ ....
○ ....
○ ....
○ ....

Health Goals for the week

○ ....
○ ....
○ ....
○ ....

Personal Goals for the week

○ ....
○ ....
○ ....
○ ....

Love Goals for the week

○ ....
○ ....
○ ....
○ ....

Financial Goals for the week

○ ....
○ ....
○ ....
○ ....

Family Goals for the week

○ ....
○ ....
○ ....
○ ....

 TO START   ⊘ COMPLETED   → CONTINUE   ⊘ STUCK   ⊗ CANCEL

Day 253

_____
_____
_____
_____
_____
_____
_____
_____

Day 254

_____
_____
_____
_____
_____
_____
_____
_____

Day 255

_____

_____

_____

_____

_____

_____

_____

_____

_____

Day 256

_____

_____

_____

_____

_____

_____

_____

_____

_____

Day 257

_____

_____

_____

_____

_____

_____

_____

_____

Day 258

_____

_____

_____

_____

_____

_____

_____

_____

Day 259

the
PEACE DOCTOR'S
*Play*book

Week 38

"Every day when you look in the mirror, take time to reconnect your heart to your soul. Don't allow the destruction of society to slip inside your home. Keep it true! Your word and your character should mean something, especially to you."

In a world full of distractions and negativity, staying true to your values and character is essential. Each day, the mirror is more than a reflection; it's a checkpoint to align your actions with your inner truth. Don't let the chaos outside invade the sanctuary of your home and heart. Protect your essence, honor your commitments, and live with integrity that begins with you. Keeping it true is not just about how others see you—it's about the respect you cultivate for yourself.

Tool:
1. Mirror Affirmation Ritual

Each morning, stand in front of the mirror and say, "I honor my word, protect my peace, and live with integrity." Take a deep breath, reconnect with your purpose, and let this guide your day.

2. Home and Character Alignment

Reflect weekly on how your actions and your home's energy align with your values. Remove negativity, set boundaries, and ensure your word and character consistently reflect your true essence.

the PEACE DOCTOR'S Playbook

Professional Goals for the week

- ○ _____
- ○ _____
- ○ _____
- ○ _____

Health Goals for the week

- ○ _____
- ○ _____
- ○ _____
- ○ _____

Personal Goals for the week

- ○ _____
- ○ _____
- ○ _____
- ○ _____

Love Goals for the week

- ○ _____
- ○ _____
- ○ _____
- ○ _____

Financial Goals for the week

- ○ _____
- ○ _____
- ○ _____
- ○ _____

Family Goals for the week

- ○ _____
- ○ _____
- ○ _____
- ○ _____

 TO START  COMPLETED   CONTINUE STUCK   CANCEL

Day 260

_____

_____

_____

_____

_____

_____

_____

_____

Day 261

_____

_____

_____

_____

_____

_____

_____

_____

Day 262

_____
_____
_____
_____
_____
_____
_____
_____
_____

Day 263

_____
_____
_____
_____
_____
_____
_____
_____
_____

Day 264

_____
_____
_____
_____
_____
_____
_____
_____
_____

Day 265

_____
_____
_____
_____
_____
_____
_____
_____
_____

Day 266

_____

_____

_____

_____

_____

_____

_____

_____

_____

the PEACE DOCTOR'S Playbook

"Teach others as you climb; share your knowledge freely."

Tools:
1. Quick Wisdom Drops

Action: *Choose one day each week to send a simple, inspiring message, resource, or lesson to someone in your circle. It could be a text, a voice note, or a quick share on social media. It's a way to uplift others without draining yourself.*

2. Open-Door Policy

Action: *Let people know they can reach out if they need advice or support. Instead of scheduling regular mentorship meetings, keep it organic. This way, you're there to guide when they need it without adding extra to your calendar.*

3. Shared Learning Moments

Action: *The next time you learn something valuable—whether it's a new skill, a podcast you listened to, or a lesson from your own experience—share it with a small group. It can be a quick "Hey, I learned this today and thought it might help you too" message. No extra work, just sharing what you're already learning.*

These tools are about keeping the flow of knowledge and support going, without feeling like you're adding another layer of work to your day. It's about planting seeds that grow organically.

Professional Goals for the week

○ _____
○ _____
○ _____
○ _____

Health Goals for the week

○ _____
○ _____
○ _____
○ _____

Personal Goals for the week

○ _____
○ _____
○ _____
○ _____

Love Goals for the week

○ _____
○ _____
○ _____
○ _____

Financial Goals for the week

○ _____
○ _____
○ _____
○ _____

Family Goals for the week

○ _____
○ _____
○ _____
○ _____

◉ TO START   ⊘ COMPLETED   ⊙→ CONTINUE   ⊘ STUCK   ⊗ CANCEL

Day 267

_____
_____
_____
_____
_____
_____
_____
_____

Day 268

_____
_____
_____
_____
_____
_____
_____
_____

Day 269

_____
_____
_____
_____
_____
_____
_____
_____

Day 270

_____
_____
_____
_____
_____
_____
_____
_____

Day 271

_____
_____
_____
_____
_____
_____
_____

Day 272

_____
_____
_____
_____
_____
_____
_____
_____

Day 273

_____

_____

_____

_____

_____

_____

_____

_____

_____

Final Notes
End of Quarter Three

What have you accomplished? What do you still need to work on?

_____

_____

_____

_____

_____

_____

_____

_____

_____

_____

_____

_____

_____

_____

_____

_____

_____

Peace is a
LIFESTYLE

QUARTER FOUR

the PEACE DOCTOR'S Playbook

"Your peace is my peace. Heal your heart, transform your soul, and ripple love into the world."

True peace begins within. Take a moment each day to check your heart and soul—how you feel, how you treat others, and how you speak to yourself. The energy you carry impacts everyone around you, from your household to your workspace. Don't let your pain overshadow others' joy. Instead, practice gratitude, embrace stillness, and commit to small acts of kindness that uplift and connect. Healing yourself is the first step to healing the world.

Tool: Soul and Peace Reflection

Start with a daily soul check: Reflect on your feelings and how you're showing up for yourself and others.

Identify one action—listening, helping, or sharing kindness—that spreads positivity to those around you.

Practice gratitude and moments of stillness to realign with your inner peace.

Transform your heart, nurture your soul, and create a ripple effect of love and peace in the lives you touch.

Professional Goals for the week

○ _____
○ _____
○ _____
○ _____

Health Goals for the week

○ _____
○ _____
○ _____
○ _____

Personal Goals for the week

○ _____
○ _____
○ _____
○ _____

Love Goals for the week

○ _____
○ _____
○ _____
○ _____

Financial Goals for the week

○ _____
○ _____
○ _____
○ _____

Family Goals for the week

○ _____
○ _____
○ _____
○ _____

◉ TO START   ⊘ COMPLETED   ⊖ CONTINUE   ⊘ STUCK   ⊗ CANCEL

Day 274

_____
_____
_____
_____
_____
_____
_____
_____
_____

Day 275

_____
_____
_____
_____
_____
_____
_____
_____
_____

Day 276

_____
_____
_____
_____
_____
_____
_____
_____

Day 277

_____
_____
_____
_____
_____
_____
_____
_____

Day 278

_____
_____
_____
_____
_____
_____
_____
_____
_____

Day 279

_____
_____
_____
_____
_____
_____
_____
_____
_____

Day 280

the PEACE DOCTOR'S
Playbook

Week 41

**"Self-care is an essential tool for your wellbeing.
Do not make anything more important than your wellness."**

I know what it's like to run yourself into the ground trying to save everyone else. I hit that wall so hard I almost didn't get back up. But here's the truth: you can't save the world if you're destroying yourself in the process. You have to believe in you.

Love yourself first—because if you're not taking care of you, what's left to give? And don't feel guilty for taking time to enjoy your life. Self-care isn't selfish; it's how you stay strong enough to keep fighting for what matters. Taking action for yourself isn't just survival—it breathes life back into your spirit.

Tool: Self-Care Action Plan
1. Prioritize Yourself

Start small. Schedule time for something that makes you feel alive—whether it's a walk, a long bath, or just sitting in peace. Let it be non-negotiable.

2. Breathwork & Reflection

Dedicate 5-10 minutes daily to just breathe. Deep breathing calms your mind and recharges your energy. Reflect on how this simple practice makes you feel.

3. Do What Brings You Joy

Each week, do one thing purely for your happiness. Whether it's dancing, reading, or being with loved ones, let it fill your cup. Remember, taking care of yourself is how you show up better for others.

the PEACE DOCTOR'S Playbook

Professional Goals for the week

○ _____
○ _____
○ _____
○ _____

Health Goals for the week

_____ ○
_____ ○
_____ ○
_____ ○

Personal Goals for the week

○ _____
○ _____
○ _____
○ _____

Love Goals for the week

_____ ○
_____ ○
_____ ○
_____ ○

Financial Goals for the week

○ _____
○ _____
○ _____
○ _____

Family Goals for the week

_____ ○
_____ ○
_____ ○
_____ ○

◉ TO START   ⊘ COMPLETED   ⊖ CONTINUE   ⊘ STUCK   ⊗ CANCEL

Day 281

Day 282

Day 283

_____
_____
_____
_____
_____
_____
_____
_____

Day 284

_____
_____
_____
_____
_____
_____
_____
_____

Day 285

_____
_____
_____
_____
_____
_____
_____
_____
_____

Day 286

_____
_____
_____
_____
_____
_____
_____
_____
_____

Day 287

the PEACE DOCTOR'S Playbook

"Focus on being productive, not just busy."
All Motion is Not Forward Motion...

It's easy to get caught up in doing a million things, thinking you're making progress—but just being busy isn't the same as being productive. Activity without purpose will burn you out fast. If you're not moving with intention, you're just spinning your wheels. Focus on what truly matters and put your energy into actions that create real impact. It's not about how much you do, but how effective you are in moving forward.

Tool: Productivity Audit
1. Evaluate Your Day

At the end of each day, write down the tasks you completed. Which ones actually moved you closer to your goals?

2. Prioritize Impact

Identify 2-3 key actions for the next day that will have the most meaningful impact. Focus on those first before getting caught up in the small stuff.

3. Cut the Clutter

Eliminate or delegate tasks that drain your energy but don't add value. Free up your time for what truly matters.

Professional Goals for the week

○ _____ ○
○ _____ ○
○ _____ ○
○ _____ ○

Health Goals for the week

○ _____ ○
○ _____ ○
○ _____ ○
○ _____ ○

Personal Goals for the week

○ _____ ○
○ _____ ○
○ _____ ○
○ _____ ○

Love Goals for the week

○ _____ ○
○ _____ ○
○ _____ ○
○ _____ ○

Financial Goals for the week

○ _____ ○
○ _____ ○
○ _____ ○
○ _____ ○

Family Goals for the week

○ _____ ○
○ _____ ○
○ _____ ○
○ _____ ○

◉ TO START   ⊘ COMPLETED   ⊝ CONTINUE   ⊘ STUCK   ⊗ CANCEL

Day 288

Day 289

Week 42

Day 290

_____
_____
_____
_____
_____
_____
_____
_____

Day 291

_____
_____
_____
_____
_____
_____
_____
_____

Day 292

_____
_____
_____
_____
_____
_____
_____
_____
_____

Day 293

_____
_____
_____
_____
_____
_____
_____
_____
_____

Day 294

**"Every ending is a chance for a new beginning.
Don't be afraid to start again."**

*Listen, life is full of cycles. Sometimes, things fall apart—it's real, it's raw, it
hurts. But that's not the end of your story; it's just the setup for the next
chapter. Don't get stuck thinking it's over just because one door closed. I've
been there, hit rock bottom, thought it was a wrap. But nah, that's where the
real growth begins. Don't let fear keep you from stepping into something
new. Every time you start again, you're leveling up, getting closer to your
greatness. It's never too late to flip the script.*

Tool: New Beginnings Checklist
1. Reflect & Release

*Sit with yourself and be real—what did that last chapter teach you? Write
down those lessons, then let that baggage go. You ain't carrying that into
your new season.*

2. Make a Move

*Don't overthink it—pick one thing you can do today to get back in the game.
Send that text, take that step, whatever it is. Just start moving.*

3. Visualize & Manifest

*Close your eyes, see yourself thriving in this next chapter. Feel that energy,
that new vibe. Let it fuel you. Every setback is just a setup for a comeback, so
lean into it and own your new beginning.*

the PEACE DOCTOR'S Playbook

Professional Goals for the week

- ○ _____
- ○ _____
- ○ _____
- ○ _____

Health Goals for the week

- _____ ○
- _____ ○
- _____ ○
- _____ ○

Personal Goals for the week

- ○ _____
- ○ _____
- ○ _____
- ○ _____

Love Goals for the week

- _____ ○
- _____ ○
- _____ ○
- _____ ○

Financial Goals for the week

- ○ _____
- ○ _____
- ○ _____
- ○ _____

Family Goals for the week

- _____ ○
- _____ ○
- _____ ○
- _____ ○

◉ TO START   ⊘ COMPLETED   ⊙ CONTINUE   ⊘ STUCK   ⊗ CANCEL

Day 295

_____
_____
_____
_____
_____
_____
_____
_____
_____

Day 296

_____
_____
_____
_____
_____
_____
_____
_____
_____

Day 297

_____
_____
_____
_____
_____
_____
_____
_____

Day 298

_____
_____
_____
_____
_____
_____
_____
_____

Day 299

_____

_____

_____

_____

_____

_____

_____

_____

Day 300

_____

_____

_____

_____

_____

_____

_____

_____

Day 301

the **PEACE DOCTOR'S** *Pla*ybook

"No one has all the answers, but together we solve the problem."
In this work for peace, we know it's not about one person having all the answers—it's about coming together. We've saved lives, healed pain, and built movements not alone, but as a community. It's about using our collective wisdom, our lived experiences, and our passion to make real change. Alone, it's heavy. Together, we become unstoppable.

Tool: Solution Circles for Community Growth
1. Build Your Ecosystem
*Connect with folks in your circle—friends, family, neighbors.
Create a space to share ideas and support each other, even if it's just a quick group chat or a monthly meet-up.*

2. Collaborate on Solutions
*When a challenge comes up, brainstorm together.
Everyone brings something to the table. It doesn't have to be formal—just share, support, and lift each other up.*

3. Celebrate the Wins
*After each effort, acknowledge the progress.
Whether it's small or big, every step forward is a victory. This is how we build our communities stronger—together.*

the PEACE DOCTOR'S
*Pla*book

Professional Goals for the week

○ _____
○ _____
○ _____
○ _____

Health Goals for the week

_____ ○
_____ ○
_____ ○
_____ ○

Personal Goals for the week

○ _____
○ _____
○ _____
○ _____

Love Goals for the week

_____ ○
_____ ○
_____ ○
_____ ○

Financial Goals for the week

○ _____
○ _____
○ _____
○ _____

Family Goals for the week

_____ ○
_____ ○
_____ ○
_____ ○

◉ TO START   ⊘ COMPLETED   ⊖ CONTINUE   ⊘ STUCK   ⊗ CANCEL

Week 44

Day 302

_____
_____
_____
_____
_____
_____
_____
_____

Day 303

_____
_____
_____
_____
_____
_____
_____
_____

Day 304

_____
_____
_____
_____
_____
_____
_____
_____

Day 305

_____
_____
_____
_____
_____
_____
_____
_____

Day 306

_____
_____
_____
_____
_____
_____
_____
_____
_____
_____

Day 307

_____
_____
_____
_____
_____
_____
_____
_____
_____
_____

Day 308

_____
_____
_____
_____
_____
_____
_____
_____
_____

"Release envy; celebrate the success of others."
Comparison is a trap. When you're too busy looking at what someone else has, you lose sight of your own blessings and progress. Envy only weighs you down and stops you from appreciating your journey. Instead, celebrate others' wins, knowing that what's meant for you is already on its way. When you uplift others, you create more space for abundance in your own life.

Tool: Gratitude & Celebration Practice
1. Shift Your Focus
When you catch yourself comparing, pause. Take a moment to write down three things you're grateful for in your life right now.

2. Celebrate Out Loud
When someone you know achieves something great, genuinely congratulate them. Send a quick message, make a call, or simply express your happiness for them. It uplifts your spirit too.

3. Reflect on Your Journey
Once a week, take 5 minutes to acknowledge your own progress. Focus on how far you've come. Remember, your path is unique, and what's meant for you will find you.

the PEACE DOCTOR'S
*Pla*book

Professional Goals for the week

○ _____
○ _____
○ _____
○ _____

Health Goals for the week

_____ ○
_____ ○
_____ ○
_____ ○

Personal Goals for the week

○ _____
○ _____
○ _____
○ _____

Love Goals for the week

_____ ○
_____ ○
_____ ○
_____ ○

Financial Goals for the week

○ _____
○ _____
○ _____
○ _____

Family Goals for the week

_____ ○
_____ ○
_____ ○
_____ ○

◉ TO START   ⊘ COMPLETED   ⊖ CONTINUE   ⊘ STUCK   ⊗ CANCEL

Day 309

_____

_____

_____

_____

_____

_____

_____

_____

_____

Day 310

_____

_____

_____

_____

_____

_____

_____

_____

_____

Day 311

_____
_____
_____
_____
_____
_____
_____
_____

Day 312

_____
_____
_____
_____
_____
_____
_____
_____

Day 313

_____

_____

_____

_____

_____

_____

_____

_____

_____

Day 314

_____

_____

_____

_____

_____

_____

_____

_____

_____

Day 315

_____

_____

_____

_____

_____

_____

_____

_____

_____

the PEACE DOCTOR'S Playbook

Week 46

"Be the light in someone's dark day."

Sometimes, the smallest acts can make the biggest difference. You never know who's struggling, who feels unseen, who's one kind word away from giving up. By simply showing up with love, with positivity, you can be the light that brightens someone's darkness. It doesn't take much—a genuine smile, a thoughtful compliment, or just listening can turn someone's whole day around. Every little bit of light you share matters.

Tool: Light-Spreading Challenge
1. Daily Light Drops

Each day, make it a point to lift someone's spirit. It could be something as simple as a heartfelt compliment, sending a text to check on someone, or giving a genuine smile to a stranger.

2. Intentional Moments

Set a reminder on your phone or calendar to pause and spread some light. It only takes a moment, but the impact can be life-changing.

3. Reflect & Recharge

At the end of each week, take a few minutes to think about the positive moments you created. Notice how being the light for others lifts your spirit too.

the **PEACE DOCTOR'S**
Playbook

Professional Goals for the week

- ○ _____
- ○ _____
- ○ _____
- ○ _____

Health Goals for the week

- _____ ○
- _____ ○
- _____ ○
- _____ ○

Personal Goals for the week

- ○ _____
- ○ _____
- ○ _____
- ○ _____

Love Goals for the week

- _____ ○
- _____ ○
- _____ ○
- _____ ○

Financial Goals for the week

- ○ _____
- ○ _____
- ○ _____
- ○ _____

Family Goals for the week

- _____ ○
- _____ ○
- _____ ○
- _____ ○

◉ TO START   ⊘ COMPLETED   ⊖ CONTINUE   ⊘ STUCK   ⊗ CANCEL

Day 316

_____

_____

_____

_____

_____

_____

_____

_____

Day 317

_____

_____

_____

_____

_____

_____

_____

_____

Day 318

_____
_____
_____
_____
_____
_____
_____
_____

Day 319

_____
_____
_____
_____
_____
_____
_____
_____

Day 320

_____
_____
_____
_____
_____
_____
_____
_____
_____

Day 321

_____
_____
_____
_____
_____
_____
_____
_____
_____

Day 322

_____

_____

_____

_____

_____

_____

_____

_____

_____

the PEACE DOCTOR'S Playbook

"**Surround yourself with people who challenge you to be better.**"
Your circle matters. If you're trying to level up, you can't hang around folks who keep you in the same place. Your people should inspire you, push you, make you uncomfortable enough to grow. You need those who will check you, hold you accountable, and remind you of your greatness when you forget. If they're not adding to your growth, they're holding you back.

Tool: Support Network Evaluation
1. Check Your Circle
Write down the names of the people you spend the most time with. Do they push you forward or pull you back? Be real with yourself.

2. Reach Out with Purpose
Identify 2-3 people who inspire you to be better. Hit them up—grab coffee, schedule a call, or just check in. Keep that connection strong.

3. Let Go to Grow
If someone's energy is draining you, it might be time to distance yourself. You don't need to cut people off harshly, but protect your space. Surround yourself with those who want to see you win.

the PEACE DOCTOR'S *Play*book

Professional Goals for the week

○ _____
○ _____
○ _____
○ _____

Health Goals for the week

_____ ○
_____ ○
_____ ○
_____ ○

Personal Goals for the week

○ _____
○ _____
○ _____
○ _____

Love Goals for the week

_____ ○
_____ ○
_____ ○
_____ ○

Financial Goals for the week

○ _____
○ _____
○ _____
○ _____

Family Goals for the week

_____ ○
_____ ○
_____ ○
_____ ○

◉ TO START ⊘ COMPLETED ⊖ CONTINUE ⊘ STUCK ⊗ CANCEL

Day 323

Day 324

Day 325

Day 326

Day 327

_____

_____

_____

_____

_____

_____

_____

_____

_____

Day 328

_____

_____

_____

_____

_____

_____

_____

_____

_____

Day 329

Week 48

**"Believe everyone is doing the best they can
with the tools they have."**

*Speak life into others. Don't judge, don't tear down, don't make people feel
small. Everyone's out here trying to make it with what they've got. Our job is
to empower—not just others, but ourselves too. Every day is another chance
to uplift, to show grace, and to correct the mistakes of yesterday. Choose to
focus on people's strengths. Highlight what's good, what's working. Let your
words be like bright flowers that lift spirits. You never know whose life you
might change just by showing love.*

Tool: Empowerment Conversation Practice
1. Model Positive Communication

*Lead by example. Challenge yourself to have one uplifting conversation this
week where you acknowledge someone's strengths. Focus on what's
working before addressing what can improve.*

2. Encourage Acts of Empowerment

*You don't need a set schedule—just be intentional. Maybe this week, or next
week, reach out to someone who could use encouragement. Share a word of
support or just check in. Be that example.*

3. Personal Practice

*Do the same for yourself. Speak life into your own journey. Take a moment
each week—or whenever you feel called—to affirm the progress you've
made. Empowerment starts with how you treat yourself and those around
you.*

the PEACE DOCTOR'S
Playbook

Professional Goals for the week

○ _____
○ _____
○ _____
○ _____

Health Goals for the week

_____ ○
_____ ○
_____ ○
_____ ○

Personal Goals for the week

○ _____
○ _____
○ _____
○ _____

Love Goals for the week

_____ ○
_____ ○
_____ ○
_____ ○

Financial Goals for the week

○ _____
○ _____
○ _____
○ _____

Family Goals for the week

_____ ○
_____ ○
_____ ○
_____ ○

◉ TO START   ⊘ COMPLETED   ⊝ CONTINUE   ⊘ STUCK   ⊗ CANCEL

Day 330

Day 331

Day 332

_____
_____
_____
_____
_____
_____
_____
_____

Day 333

_____
_____
_____
_____
_____
_____
_____
_____

Day 334

_____
_____
_____
_____
_____
_____
_____
_____
_____

Day 335

_____
_____
_____
_____
_____
_____
_____
_____
_____

Day 336

the
PEACE DOCTOR'S
Playbook

Week 49

"Greatness is your destiny—step into it, break through, and make an impact every day."

You don't need permission, a big stage, or anyone's approval to be great. Greatness begins with how you show up daily—disciplined, prepared, and focused. Life's challenges aren't breaking you; they're shaping you for breakthroughs. Every small action, whether helping someone or pursuing your dreams, contributes to the bigger picture of your greatness.

Tool: Greatness Blueprint

Daily Discipline: Set one bold goal each day and execute it with focus and care.

Impact Tracker: Record small acts of kindness or progress that create ripples of positivity.

Reflection Time: Reflect on past challenges and how they've led to growth. Use those lessons to guide your actions today.

Live intentionally.
Prepare, execute, and embrace your greatness—because it's already within you.

the PEACE DOCTOR'S
Playbook

Professional Goals for the week

- ○ _____
- ○ _____
- ○ _____
- ○ _____

Health Goals for the week

- _____ ○
- _____ ○
- _____ ○
- _____ ○

Personal Goals for the week

- ○ _____
- ○ _____
- ○ _____
- ○ _____

Love Goals for the week

- _____ ○
- _____ ○
- _____ ○
- _____ ○

Financial Goals for the week

- ○ _____
- ○ _____
- ○ _____
- ○ _____

Family Goals for the week

- _____ ○
- _____ ○
- _____ ○
- _____ ○

◉ TO START   ⊘ COMPLETED   → CONTINUE   ⊘ STUCK   ⊗ CANCEL

Day 337

_____
_____
_____
_____
_____
_____
_____
_____

Day 338

_____
_____
_____
_____
_____
_____
_____
_____

Day 339

_____
_____
_____
_____
_____
_____
_____
_____
_____

Day 340

_____
_____
_____
_____
_____
_____
_____
_____
_____

Day 341

Day 342

Day 343

_____

_____

_____

_____

_____

_____

_____

_____

the PEACE DOCTOR'S
Playbook

"Value consistency; it builds trust and credibility." "Be consistent in someone else's life; watch how it transforms them—and you."

Consistency isn't just about what you do for yourself—it's about showing up for others, again and again. True impact happens when you make someone feel seen, valued, and supported. Whether it's checking in on a friend, reading with your child every week, or simply sending a message to say, "I'm here for you," these small, consistent actions build trust and deepen relationships. The real magic happens when you show up, not just once, but over and over. That's how you change lives, and in turn, change your own.

Action Tool: Consistency Connection Project
1. Choose Your People

Select 3-5 individuals you want to be more consistent for—a friend, mentee, family member, or even a neighbor. Commit to being a steady presence in their life.

2. Consistency Plan

- **Weekly Check-Ins:** *Every week, send a simple message, make a call, or stop by to show you care.*
- **Set a Ritual:** *Pick one consistent activity, like a Tuesday night story time with your child or a monthly lunch with a friend.*

3. Track the Impact

Use your journal to note any changes in their responses or your relationship. Reflect on how showing up consistently strengthens your bond and the support you both feel. Consistency isn't just a habit; it's a lifeline. Be that lifeline for someone else, and watch how it builds them up—and transforms you in the process.

Professional Goals for the week

○ _____
○ _____
○ _____
○ _____

Health Goals for the week

_____ ○
_____ ○
_____ ○
_____ ○

Personal Goals for the week

○ _____
○ _____
○ _____
○ _____

Love Goals for the week

_____ ○
_____ ○
_____ ○
_____ ○

Financial Goals for the week

○ _____
○ _____
○ _____
○ _____

Family Goals for the week

_____ ○
_____ ○
_____ ○
_____ ○

◉ TO START   ⊘ COMPLETED   ⊝ CONTINUE   ⊘ STUCK   ⊗ CANCEL

Day 344

_____
_____
_____
_____
_____
_____
_____
_____
_____

Day 345

_____
_____
_____
_____
_____
_____
_____
_____
_____

Day 346

_____
_____
_____
_____
_____
_____
_____
_____

Day 347

_____
_____
_____
_____
_____
_____
_____
_____

Day 348

_____

_____

_____

_____

_____

_____

_____

_____

_____

Day 349

_____

_____

_____

_____

_____

_____

_____

_____

_____

Day 350

the **PEACE DOCTOR'S** *Playbook*

"Empower others; do not create co-dependency."

Listen, real power is about building people up so they can stand on their own. I've been doing this work for years—on these streets, in our schools, in our communities. I'm not here to hold your hand forever; I'm here to teach you to walk, run, and then sprint on your own. We're not raising followers—we're raising leaders.

You want change? You've got to give people the tools to think for themselves. It's not enough to keep giving out answers—you've got to teach them how to ask the right questions, how to move on their own two feet. That's how we break cycles. That's how we build a community that doesn't just survive but thrives.

Tool: Capacity-Building Actions
1. Skill Up

Teach skills that build independence. Help people see they've got what it takes to lead.

2. Learn Together

Don't just teach—learn with your people.
Grow together, challenge each other, build that real strength.

3. Push Forward

Encourage your kids, your crew, your community to step up and take charge. Let them find their own power, their own voice. That's how we rise.

the PEACE DOCTOR'S Playbook

Professional Goals for the week

- ○ _____
- ○ _____
- ○ _____
- ○ _____

Health Goals for the week

- ○ _____
- ○ _____
- ○ _____
- ○ _____

Personal Goals for the week

- ○ _____
- ○ _____
- ○ _____
- ○ _____

Love Goals for the week

- ○ _____
- ○ _____
- ○ _____
- ○ _____

Financial Goals for the week

- ○ _____
- ○ _____
- ○ _____
- ○ _____

Family Goals for the week

- ○ _____
- ○ _____
- ○ _____
- ○ _____

◉ TO START   ✓ COMPLETED   CONTINUE   STUCK   CANCEL

Day 352

_____

_____

_____

_____

_____

_____

_____

_____

_____

Day 353

_____

_____

_____

_____

_____

_____

_____

_____

_____

Day 354

_____

_____

_____

_____

_____

_____

_____

_____

Peace is a
LIFESTYLE

Day 355

_____

_____

_____

_____

_____

_____

_____

_____

Day 356

_____
_____
_____
_____
_____
_____
_____
_____
_____

Day 357

_____
_____
_____
_____
_____
_____
_____
_____
_____

Day 358

the PEACE DOCTOR'S
Playbook

"Live every day fully; make joy a part of your routine."

Listen, I get it. Life can feel heavy—especially when you're just trying to survive. But hear me: you can't let the weight of the world steal your joy. You can't stay stuck on that same corner, that same block, feeling like there's nothing more out there for you. Life is bigger than that. You've got to take back your power, and that starts with finding your joy.

This world? It's your classroom. It's where you learn, where you grow, where you discover who you really are. Don't let it pass you by. Wake up every day and find that one thing that makes you smile, that reminds you why you're still fighting. Even if it's just sitting on your stoop and feeling the sun on your face, do it. Make joy your rebellion. Make joy your weapon. You are not just surviving—you're living, and that's your victory.

the
PEACE DOCTOR'S
Playbook

Tool: Daily Joy List
1. Name Your Joy

We made it to the end of the year!
Think about all the moments of joy and how they made you feel. What's
one thing that makes you feel good? Is it writing rhymes? Playing ball?
Just chilling with your people? Write it down. That's your power—own it.

2. Make It a Ritual

Pick one thing from that list and commit to doing it every day.
Even if it's just for 10 minutes. Let that joy remind you that you're alive,
that you're more than your block.

3. Reflect & Own Your Growth

At the end of each week, think about how those moments of joy made you
feel. Did they change your day, your vibe? That's the beginning of
something bigger—your growth, your story. You've got more in you than
you think, but you've got to let yourself feel it first.

the PEACE DOCTOR'S
Playbook

Professional Goals for the week

- ○ _____
- ○ _____
- ○ _____
- ○ _____

Health Goals for the week

- _____ ○
- _____ ○
- _____ ○
- _____ ○

Personal Goals for the week

- ○ _____
- ○ _____
- ○ _____
- ○ _____

Love Goals for the week

- _____ ○
- _____ ○
- _____ ○
- _____ ○

Financial Goals for the week

- ○ _____
- ○ _____
- ○ _____
- ○ _____

Family Goals for the week

- _____ ○
- _____ ○
- _____ ○
- _____ ○

◉ TO START   ⊘ COMPLETED   ⊖ CONTINUE   ⊘ STUCK   ⊗ CANCEL

Day 359

_____
_____
_____
_____
_____
_____
_____
_____

Day 360

_____
_____
_____
_____
_____
_____
_____
_____

Day 361

_____

_____

_____

_____

_____

_____

_____

_____

_____

Day 362

_____

_____

_____

_____

_____

_____

_____

_____

_____

Day 363

_____
_____
_____
_____
_____
_____
_____
_____
_____

Day 364

_____
_____
_____
_____
_____
_____
_____
_____
_____

Day 365

_____

_____

_____

_____

_____

_____

_____

_____

_____

the PEACE DOCTOR'S
Playbook

Final Notes:
End of Quarter Four

What have you accomplished? What do you still need to work on?

Peace in
LIFESTYLE

the PEACE DOCTOR'S Playbook

"Personal stories from people The Peace Doctor directly impacted and the quotes I said that inspired them to do something different."
-Erica Ford, The Peace Doctor

"Kill the pessimist in myself, stop engaging with the chatter in my head and believe and understand and commit to the idea that everything everything is possible with time and dedication we can make it happen."
-David Huie $2 Dave, The Great Connector

"*I remember one day we went to take your mom to the doctor and we were discussing teen parties and you suggested doing it at Roy Wilkens. I was so against it, I was like that's a family center, teens aint gonna wanna party at a family center and you said they will come if you make them come…and the rest is history."*
-Tamara L. Simmons

"You have to take yourself out of it."
"You have to communicate better and lead from 30, 000 feet."
& "I will not accept mediocrity."
-AU Hogan LIFE Camp's Chief of Street, Actor, 2x Golden Globe Champ

"STRAIGHT AHEAD!"
The reason why. I love when you say this because it's a instant reminder no matter the challenges, success or adversity. We having to keep moving forward. Detach from what you been through or going through see the blessing ahead straight head.
-Jaytaun McMillian Urban Yogi

"Now tell your story" is a quote from you that rings in my brain…
it's the quote that lead me to make pain on beats. You said this to me when you brought me food and a notebook to the hospital and rest is history.
-Ceillise C3 Craig one of the worlds top battle rappers

the PEACE DOCTOR'S Playbook

"Personal stories from people The Peace Doctor directly impacted and the quotes I said that inspired them to do something different."
-Erica Ford, The Peace Doctor

"Nature is unforgiving to those who don't pay attention to details"
This has inspired me to think deeply about my actions. Going through life haphazardly is not cool, but stopping and being intentional with everything you do is where you will feel more fulfilled and live a more fruitful life.
-Tyla Ford 3rd Grade teacher & my oldest niece

"Get the knowledge"
The impact of this quote for me revealed that you can be smart and knowledgeable in one area but it does not necessarily apply to all areas. Having experiences in leadership do not make you a leader in all situations.
&
"You have to have the right people"-a good fit is not only about resume and relationship. Organizations can find success with putting the right people in place.
-NYC DOE former Principal Omotayo Cienus

"We can not continue to wait for others to come in and save our communities.
We must save ourselves. We cannot expect for others to validate our work. Some of the things we do are non-traditional and isn't represented in the data they collect."
-Chico Tillmon, Director of Community Violence
Intervention Leadership Academy at University of Chicago

the
PEACE DOCTOR'S
Playbook

"Personal stories from people The Peace Doctor directly impacted and the quotes I said that inspired them to do something different."
-Erica Ford, The Peace Doctor

Vanessa and Nicole were talking and you came up. She said y'all went to a retreat and you said to "stop hiding behind yourself mask." Her take away is that we always hide behind our pain so we don't have to reveal our real selves.
-Two leaders in the CVI world based in NYC
both leading gun violence prevention groups

The most valuable thing I've learned from you isn't a quote, it's a mindset—embracing peace as a lifestyle. Peace for me is peace of mind and your wellness journey has opened my eyes to my own journey. I've embraced peace of mind as a lifestyle because you embody it and I've gained a lot of clarity as a result.
-Rachel Noerdlinger

"I Love My LIFE" is one of Erica's most inspirational quotes in my life. It's more than just a motto — it's a transformative affirmation that, when spoken aloud, rewires the brain, helping us see every challenge and moment as part of a greater good. By declaring love for life, we align with its inherent value, cultivating resilience, gratitude, and the belief that all experiences shape us for our highest purpose.
-Kheperah Kearse Chief Wellness Officer LIFE Camp

I remember my first thoughts when you were on stage in Aspen for lead with love . You were talking about your community and how you all have to take responsibility in transforming your community from w/in. How you thought yoga was just for white people and you challenged Deepak Chopra to bring the Urban Yogis to Queens. Just how passionate you were on stage with your crazy hair and presence. It was different, you were coming from a place of knowing what needed to happen and not be in victim mentality. I remember walking up to you after and that's when I started following you to watch your journey and the rest is history ..
-Victoria Smith "Teach a Man to Fish"

"*Save The Babies*"

Some statements are not necessarily original, but take on profound meaning when repeated at a particular time by a special person. Erica Ford not only had a love for a generation of our youth, more important, she made that a life's work. She inspired me to help her design a T-Shirt with pictures of over 20 Black youths murdered by street violence and design the Life Camp logo. An early member of the December 12th Movement, and although taking different paths, we both continue that love and passion to save our youth and community. My direction through the building of the Black Men's Movement Against Crack, The African Brotherhood for Self-Determination, and our current "Stop The Killing" Campaign of the December 12th Movement. Erica, through building LIFE Camp into a local organization with a national reach.

Omowale Clay is my political father, shaping my principles and grounding me in the fight for Black liberation through his leadership and wisdom. Through the December 12th Movement, he instilled in me the power of grassroots organizing, Pan-Africanism, and unapologetic advocacy for justice, guiding every step of my journey.

Deepak Chopra says to me as i finish this journal that
"There is no way to Peace Peace is the way"
by AJ Muste is a quote he lives by and drilled in all of us!

Deepak has been influential in my journey for peace but let me tell you how I met Deepak and how he helped us go 4 yrs without a killing in our southeast target area.

I met Deepak from one of his volunteers seeing our work on social media. He followed us, became attracted to Peace week and urged Deepak's team that they needed to partner with us. I didn't know who Deepak was at that time and wasn't thinking about working with him but the universe, the ancestors brought us together we organized an event part of his ABC Home & Carpet we did a conversation on Love with Deepak, Russell Simmions & Myself and I told him that yoga & meditation ish don't work in my community it's for rich white people and he said NO it is for everyone and he would come train our mothers who lost their loved ones to gun violence & young people, we built an urban yogi's program and rest is history it worked!

Deepak Chopra

the PEACE DOCTOR'S
Playbook

"The Season's Over—Now What?"

You ran the drills.
You executed the plays.
You adapted when life threw curveballs,
fumbled a few times, and maybe even took a victory lap.

But here's the deal:
Champions don't stop when the buzzer sounds—they prepare for the next game.

This year, you
LEVELED UP.
You built peace, sharpened your strategies, and strengthened your team—you.
Now it's time to review the game tape, celebrate the wins, and strategize for next season.

Remember:
Peace isn't a one-time play; it's a lifestyle.
And just like the greats, you've got to stay in shape. Keep practicing those daily drills,
call the right plays, and make sure your bench (a.k.a. your support system) stays strong.

Coach's Final Words:
Take what you've learned and pass it on—teamwork wins games.
Keep pushing, keep healing, and keep building peace.
And above all, don't let the haters (or life) get you off your game.
The clock's reset. The ball's in your hands. What's your next move?

"You don't just play the game—you **change** it."

the PEACE DOCTOR'S
Playbook

The following books and people have inspired quotes and lessons throughout this playbook.

Paulo Coelho, The Alchemist,

Shakespeare, Merchant of Venice

Albert Humphrey, Founder of SWOT Analysis

Giant Thinking/ Bartendaz Health & Wellness Group

Amilcar Cabral

David Goggins

Michael Bernard Beckwith

M.D. Arnold

Queen Afua

Kheperah Kearse

Tara Sheahan

Viola Plummer